RA
418
'ORG

KU-014-951

ENVIRONMENTAL POLICY AND TECHNICAL CHANGE

ECONOMICS
LIBRARY
24 MAR 1986
AND STATISTICS

WITHDRAWN

ORGANISATION FOR ECONOMIC CO-OPERATION AND DEVELOPMENT

Pursuant to article 1 of the Convention signed in Paris on 14th December, 1960, and which came into force on 30th September, 1961, the Organisation for Economic Co-operation and Development (OECD) shall promote policies designed:

- to achieve the highest sustainable economic growth and employment and a rising standard of living in Member countries, while maintaining financial stability, and thus to contribute to the development of the world economy;
- to contribute to sound economic expansion in Member as well as non-member countries in the process of economic development; and
- to contribute to the expansion of world trade on a multilateral, non-discriminatory basis in accordance with international obligations.

The Signatories of the Convention on the OECD are Austria, Belgium, Canada, Denmark, France, the Federal Republic of Germany, Greece, Iceland, Ireland, Italy, Luxembourg, the Netherlands, Norway, Portugal, Spain, Sweden, Switzerland, Turkey, the United Kingdom and the United States. The following countries acceded subsequently to this Convention (the dates are those on which the instruments of accession were deposited): Japan (28th April, 1964), Finland (28th January, 1969), Australia (7th June, 1971) and New Zealand (29th May, 1973).

The Socialist Federal Republic of Yugoslavia takes part in certain work of the OECD (agreement of 28th October, 1961).

Publié en français sous le titre :

**POLITIQUE DE L'ENVIRONNEMENT
ET CHANGEMENT TECHNIQUE**

© OECD, 1985
Application for permission to reproduce or translate
all or part of this publication should be made to:
Director of Information, OECD
2, rue André-Pascal, 75775 PARIS CEDEX 16, France.

The OECD Environment Committee's programme of studies on the impact of environmental policies on technical change consisted principally in two complementary analyses ; first : to determine and analyse the characteristics of Member country environmental policies at the policy-making and enforcement stages likely to affect technological change in industry; secondly, to make detailed studies of a number of industries and firms subject to environmental regulations in order to check the impact of the parameters identified during the preceding stage. On the basis of this analysis, the present publication is an attempt to assess how and how far environmental policies and technical change in industry interact and to draw conclusions as to how environmental policies can be formulated and implemented in order to stimulate technical innovation.

This study has been carried out by the Secretariat under the supervision of the Environment Committee's Group of Economic Experts which asked for its derestriction ; it is published under the responsibility of the Secretary General.

Also available

ENVIRONMENT AND ECONOMICS. Results of the International Conference on Environment and Economics, 18th-21st June 1984 (April 1985)
(97 85 01 1) ISBN 92-64-12691-0 248 pages   £12.00   US$24.00   F120.00

THE MACRO-ECONOMIC IMPACT OF ENVIRONMENTAL EXPENDITURE (June 1985)
(97 85 06 1) ISBN 92-64-12716-X   120 pages   £7.50   US$15.00   F75.00

THE STATE OF THE ENVIRONMENT 1985 (June 1985)
(97 85 04 1) ISBN 92-64-12713-5 276 pages   £16.50   US$33.00   F165.00

OECD ENVIRONMENTAL DATA – COMPENDIUM 1985 (June 1985) bilingual
(97 85 05 3) ISBN 92-64-02678-9 298 pages   £15.00   US$30.00   F150.00

ENVIRONMENTAL EFFECTS OF ELECTRICITY GENERATION (June 1985)
(97 85 03 1) ISBN 92-64-12697-X   156 pages   £9.50   US$19.00   F95.00

TRANSFRONTIER MOVEMENTS OF HAZARDOUS WASTES. Legal and Institutional Aspects (March 1985)
(97 85 02 1) ISBN 92-64-12694-5 304 pages   £14.00   US$28.00   F140.00

Prices charged at the OECD Publications Office.

*THE OECD CATALOGUE OF PUBLICATIONS and supplements will be sent free of charge
on request addressed either to OECD Publications Office,
2, rue André-Pascal, 75775 PARIS CEDEX 16, or to the OECD Sales Agent in your country.*

TABLE OF CONTENTS

Part One

TECHNICAL CHANGE, STATE INTERVENTION
AND ECONOMIC GROWTH : AN OVERVIEW

Part One

TECHNICAL CHANGE, STATE INTERVENTION AND ECONOMIC
GROWTH : AN OVERVIEW.

Ever since environmental policies began to
achieve a certain importance, analysts have been
striving to determine their influence on the main
economic parameters such as price levels, growth,
employment and trade. These questions have been and
still are the subject of on-going analysis in the
various Member countries and within the OECD. A
more recent question is to determine to what extent
environmental policies, and more particularly
pollution control, affect technical change in
industry.

As will be seen throughout this report, this
is a many-faceted question, but before going into
detail it is necessary briefly to place the problem
in its context: what is the relative importance of
technical change in the present economic situation?
What is the scale of government intervention (which
will be referred to as "regulation") and what
influence does it have on the process of technical
change (or technological innovation)? What is the
relative importance of the environment, and more
particularly pollution control, in these
mechanisms? Only when the problem has been placed
in its context will it be possible to analyse in
detail the interrelationships between technical
change and environmental protection measures.

*The problem of the
relationship between
environment and technical
change is many-faceted
and needs to be placed
in the present economic
context.*

I.   TECHNICAL CHANGE

1.1. A key variable

Technical change, and more particularly
technological innovation, has long been considered
an essential factor in economic development even
though it is frequently treated as an "exogenous" or
"residual" variable in economic models. As a growth
factor, frequently the cause of new breakthroughs in
the case of major innovations (steam engine, loom,
etc.), technical changes stand out as landmarks in
economic history, initially occurring at a slow
rate, then at increasing speed since the industrial
revolution.

*Technical change -
mainspring of growth*

Many economists, including the most distinguished have discussed and analysed the role of technical change in economic development. It is well known that Joseph Schumpeter attached particular importance to the definition and analysis of the innovation phenomenon which he saw an essential factor in growth and a major cause of economic cycles. Schumpeter distinguishes between <u>invention</u> and <u>innovation</u>, the first being more or less a purely scientific and technological discovery, the second manifest itself through its introduction into economic activity. According to Schumpeter, innovation may appear in four different forms :

-- manufacture of a new product;

-- introduction of a new manufacturing process;

-- opening of a new market;

-- exploitation of a new source of raw materials.

Most writers subsequently more or less accepted this definition of technological innovation which is understood here as the <u>development, application and introduction on the market of a new product or process.</u> Innovation may have its origin inside or outside the firm, i.e. the firm may develop the innovation itself or may adopt and apply a technique developed by others. This definition underlines the central role of the introduction of technical change into economic activity, as stressed by Schumpeter.

In the environmental field, within this general definition, innovations made for commercial purposes ("general business innovation") have to be distinguished from those inspired entirely or partly by environmental protection regulations and the need to comply with them ("compliance innovations"). In the former case, the aim of innovation is to increase the firm's competitiveness and profitability, in the latter, its primary purpose is to ensure compliance with standards and regulations (anti-pollution technologies, for example) at the lowest possible cost.

Technical change is therefore recognised as an essential factor in economic development. This is demontrated by the acceleration of technical change after the Second World War, accompanied to the end of the sixties by rapidly rising productivity (cf. Table 1).

Schumpeter's definition - still applicable.

There are innovations for commercial ends and those made in order to comply with regulations.

Leading role of technical change in economic growth

In Japan, the Technology Planning Agency considers that the contribution of technical progress to economic growth was 20 per cent over the period 1955-60, 25 per cent for 1960-65, 38 per cent for 1965-70, and 47 per cent for 1970-72. This contribution is expected to rise to 65 per cent between 1975 and 1982 (1). For the United States, Denison (2) considers that during the period 1948-73, of the annual average increase of 2.6 per cent of national income per person employed, 1.4 per cent, i.e. over half, was due to a residual factor or "unexplained portion" which he defines as "increase in knowledge and items not classified elsewhere". Though it cannot be determined exactly, some part of this unexplained portion is, according to Denison, due to technical change.

... and beyond...

The fact is that in the post-war period there was a combination of a number of factors favourable to technological innovation, in particular the maturing of inventions developed before or during the war, the need to reconstruct the production base, the appearance of new markets and virtually unlimited potential demand. The result was an unprecedented period of innovation (1).

While technical change seems to make a vital contribution to growth, the reverse also seems to be true. A major cause of the present stagnation and economic recession could be due to a slowdown in technical progress. Denison's study shows that over the period 1973-76, national income per person employed in the United States decreased by an annual average of 0.6 per cent while the decline in national income that was due to the "unexplained portion", already mentioned, was 0.7 per cent(3).

Could the slower rate of technical progress be a cause of the current economic recession ?

It cannot be denied that with the recession which started in 1973 there was a significant levelling off in productivity growth. In some countries this fall appeared as early as the late 60s. It can be seen on table 1 that the productivity growth rate in the manufacturing sector which ranged from 3.0 to 10.7 per cent accross countries during period 1960-1973, fell to 1,7 - 6,2 per cent in 1973 - 1980. If one takes the whole economy, i.e. the GDP per employed person, the decrease is even more pronounced (the growth rate is 2 - 9 per cent in 1960 - 1970 and falls to 1 - 4 per cent in 1970-1980). However, this phenomenon cannot be solely attributed to a slowdown in technical progress, many causes have been identified, though their relative importance cannot really be quantified. Some authors even consider that to attempt to do so would be very

A central concern - the fall in productivity growth...

Table 1

CHANGES IN MANUFACTURING PRODUCTIVITY AND OUTPUT IN 11 OECD COUNTRIES, 1960-80
(annual changes in percent)

Year	United States	Canada	Japan	France	Germany	Italy	United Kingdom	Belgium	Denmark	Netherlands	Sweden
Output per hour											
1960-80	2.7	3.8	9.4	5.6	5.4	5.9	3.6	7.2	6.4	7.3	5.2
1960-73	3.0	4.5	10.7	6.0	5.5	6.9	4.3	7.0	6.4	7.6	6.7
1973-80	1.7	2.2	6.8	4.9	4.8	3.6	1.9	6.2	5.1	5.6	2.1
1974	2.4	1.6	2.4	3.5	6.0	4.9	.8	5.4	3.3	8.3	3.6
1975	2.9	2.6	3.9	3.1	4.8	4.4	2.0	5.2	10.4	1.7	-0.4
1976	4.4	4.9	9.4	8.2	6.3	8.6	4.0	10.3	7.7	12.7	1.0
1977	2.4	5.1	7.2	5.1	5.3	1.1	1.6	5.0	3.7	4.1	-1.5
1978	.9	3.1	7.9	5.3	3.8	2.9	3.2	6.0	4.4	6.0	4.3
1979	1.1	1.2	8.0	5.4	6.3	7.3	3.3	5.8	2.3	5.5	8.1
1980	-.3	-1.4	6.2	.6	-.7	6.7	.3	3.6	1.7	3.7	0.6

Source : U.S. Department of Labour, Bureau of Labour Statistics.

risky (5). Denison lists no less than ten factors, some of which have numerous sub-categories. Among the most frequently cited factors are:

-- changes in the composition of production;

-- changes in the characteristics of the labour forces;

...the causes of which are difficult to identify...

-- changes in the structure of land use and capital;

-- higher energy prices;

-- slower pace to research and development activity;

-- increased State intervention in such fields as health, industrial safety and environmental protection.

...but the central role of technical change continues to be stressed.

For the most part these factors include a technological component and affect the production function.

Nevertheless, among the causes of the decline in technological innovation, regulation is the most frequently highlighted (2,5), even though its real impact has rarely been measured. In a recent study, Christainsen and Haveman (6) estimate that regulations were responsible for 12 to 25 per cent of the decline in productivity growth recorded in the United States over the period 1958-77 (7). But this covers the whole spectrum of regulations, so that the share relating to the environment would necessarily be smaller, though still undetermined, since it varies in the ratio 1-3 according to author. Christainsen and Haveman (8), claim that 8 to 12 per cent of the drop in productivity in the United States is due to environmental regulations (9).

It is not our intention to analyse here, the causes of the fall in productivity, but it is important to note the close links between technical change and productivity, even if they are as yet little quantified, since the fall in productivity is one of the main causes of concern in the present economic situation. In other words, the problem of the relationship between environment and technical change is part of the broader problem of declining productivity growth. At this stage we could also point out that technical change is only one factor among others, determining productivity growth, but since this is our main concern it is necessary to go further back up the causal chain to identify the various factors determining technical progress and innovation.

1.2. Innovation potential

Technical change is both a cause and a result of economic development. They fertilise each other. Technological innovation stimultates economic development by increasing productivity, opening up new markets and helping to create new firms and hence jobs. Reciprocally, technological innovation needs a favourable economic, social and cultural environment if it is to develop and spread. A dynamic economy and society are essential factors for technical change. It is thus necessary to "maximise the chances that such a combination will arise" (1), i.e. to allow a true "technical culture" (10), favourable for innovation.

Innovation is an economic and cultural phenomenon and its causes are complex and manifold...

It can be seen that the factors determining innovation are numerous and their inter-relationships complex; to detail all of them would be outside the scope of this report. Nevertheless, if environmental protection influences innovation positively or negatively, this influence has to be situated in its context, i.e. related to the principle factors involved.

...the environment is only one aspect...

Five main factors influencing innovation can be distinguished (11):

-- research and development;

-- technical training;

-- diffusion of technical changes;

-- financing of innovation;

-- government intervention (regulation).

The first four factors will be discussed here; the fifth (regulation), being the general subject of the report, will be dealth with in detail below (section II of Part I, and Parts II and III).

a) Research and Development

R and D is considered to be one of the main sources of innovation, to such and extent that through the lack of other quantitative indicators technical change is sometimes measured by the yardstick of R and D expenditures. Obviously such a

14

*R-D, source of
innovation...*

procedure is not entirely justified since R and D
expenditure measures the effort made rather than the
results obtained, but while it is hardly possible to
measure its yield, R and D expenditure is
nevertheless a valuable indicator of a country's
innovation potential.

R and D expenditure certainly increased
sharply in most countries during the post-war

*...has lost momentum
during the past ten
years.*

period. Subsequent trends in the 60s and 70s are
more varied, though the general tendency is a
slowing-down in the increase or even a decline in
certain countries. Certain data are given below on
the breakdown of R and D expenditure for different
purposes such as energy, environmental protection,
defense, etc.

After having increased sharply in the
post-war period, industrial R and D was virtually

*Industry is the main
source of R-D...*

stagnant from 1967 to 1975, the main reason being
reduced public funding (5). The relative share of
industrial R and D fell from 60 per cent of total
financing in 1967 to 50 per cent in 1975.

30 to 40 per cent of R and D is financed out
of public funds, but over the period 1970-1980 the
R and D share of total public expenditure fell in

*...with governments
coming second.*

many countries. Nevertheless, now that stimulation
of technological innovation is becoming a major
objective in OECD countries, it can be expected that
with the revival in private R and D, public R and D
spending will also rise, the objective being to
increase total R and D (private and public) as a
share of GNP (1). The breakdown of publicly
financed R and D varies considerably from one
country to another.

It can be seen in Table 2 that the objectives
"defence" and "advancement of knowledge"were the
most significant. It is also worth noting the share
of R and D in the field of energy (5 to 14 per cent
according to country, 23 per cent in Italy) ; this
share has increased rapidly in almost all countries.
Public financing of industrial R and D, which had
decreased somewhat in the past, has regained
priority in some countries as part of policies to
stimulate technical innovation.

R and D in the field of environment clearly
appears a non-priority (0.6 to 2.9 per cent of total
public R and D funding in 1980 - see also table 4
and graph 2).

Table 2

PUBLIC R & D FUNDING BY SOCIO-ECONOMIC OBJECTIVES IN 1980
(IN % OF TOTAL PUBLIC R & D EXPENDITURES)

	Agriculture Forestry, Fishing	Industrial Development	Energy	Transport & Telecommuni- cations	Urban & Rural Planning	Environment (1)	Health (2)	Social Development Services	Earth & Atmosphere	Advancement of Knowledge	Civil Space	Defense
UNITED STATES	2.2	0.3	11.4	2.8	0.4	0.8	12.1	2.3	2.1	3.9	14.5	47.3
JAPAN	12.0	5.8	12.4	1.4	1.1	1.6	2.9	0.8	1.4	52.5	5.7	2.3
GERMANY	1.9	10.0	14.4	2.0	1.5	2.0	4.1	3.8	2.8	43.1	4.3	10.1
FRANCE	3.9	9.3	7.5	2.7	1.4	1.1	4.4	1.3	3.0	22.2	6.2	36.5
UNITED KINGDOM	3.7	6.6	6.3	0.4	1.0	0.9	1.1	0.9	0.7	22.5	1.8	54.1
ITALY	4.1	17.4	22.9	0.4	0.8	1.0	4.5	2.2	2.1	35.7	6.2	2.7
CANADA	20.3	12.8	11.9	6.0	0.3	1.3	7.5	5.6	5.8	21.8	-	6.8
NETHERLANDS	8.3	5.7	4.3	1.6	3.4	"	5.2	6.0	1.2	55.2	3.2	3.1
SUEDE	2.0	7.7	10.2	2.5	2.0	1.8	7.1	8.3	0.7	39.4	2.8	15.6
BELGIUM	4.8	14.9	8.7	1.4	2.0	2.9	13.	11.1	3.7	31.8	5.6	0.3
NORWAY	9.2	14.9	4.9	5.3	0.7	3.0	5.0	7.2	1.7	42.8	0.6	4.6
DENMARK	8.8	13.6	7.7	0.8	2.2	2.1	10.9	7.9	3.1	39.1	3.6	0.3
FINLAND	11.9	21.1	6.0	1.5	0.6	0.8	0.8	7.3	6.7	41.3	-	1.9
NEW-ZELAND	33.5	12.9	5.5	1.3	1.3	-	6.3	4.1	17.0	15.7	-	-
IRELAND	25.7	16.1	1.0	1.5	5.8	0.6	9.9	10.2	0.9	37.3	0.9	1.4
SPAIN	18.2	17.3	14.5	0.1	-	2.7	1.2	15.6	4.5	13.6	7.4	-
PORTUGAL	17.6	8.6	-	-	12.7	-	15.5	5.4	7.1	25.6	-	-
GREECE	23.5	5.2	10.0	-	-	-	-	9.2	5.9	30.8	0.4	6.3

Source : OECD

(1) See also Table 6
(2) excluding pollution

16

Table 3

GROSS NATIONAL EXPENDITURE ON R & D
IN COMPARISON WITH 1000 * GROSS DOMESTIC PRODUCT

	1975	1976	1977	1978	1979	1980
UNITED STATES	24.4	24.3	23.9	23.7	24.1	24.5
JAPAN	19.4	19.3	19.1	19.3	20.4	
GERMANY	22.2	21.5	21.4	22.4	22.7	
FRANCE	18.0	17.7	17.6	17.7	18.2	18.3
UNITED KINGDOM	21.2			22.0		
ITALY	9.3	8.6	8.9	8.4	8.4	
NETHERLANDS	21.2	20.7	19.9	19.7	19.8	
SWITZERLAND	24.0	24.5	22.9	24.2	24.5	
CANADA (B)	9.7	9.2	9.3	9.6	9.4	
SWEDEN	17.5		18.7		18.9	
BELGIUM	13.3		13.7		14.0	
AUSTRALIA		9.9		9.6		
DENMARK	13.4				9.7	
NORWAY	9.2		14.0	14.0	13.8	
AUSTRIA (1)	10.0					
YUGOSLAVIA			11.6			
FINLAND	9.4		10.2		10.8	
SPAIN		3.5				
NEW-ZELAND	8.6	7.6	8.2			
IRELAND (R)	8.6		8.1		7.6	
GREECE (1)		2.1	2.3	2.2	2.0	
PORTUGAL		2.7		3.2		
ICELAND	9.1		6.6			1.6

Source : O.E.C.D.

17

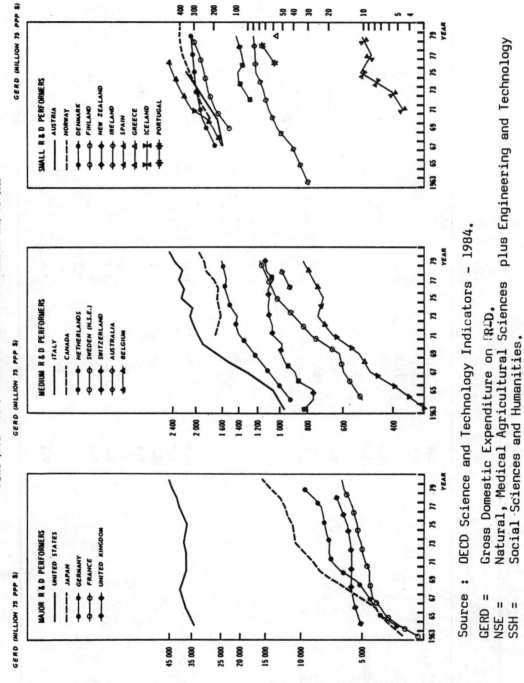

Graph 1

GERD (NSE + SSH) IN MILLION 1975 PPP US DOLLARS 1963 TO 1980

Source : OECD Science and Technology Indicators – 1984.

GERD = Gross Domestic Expenditure on R&D.
NSE = Natural, Medical Agricultural Sciences plus Engineering and Technology
SSH = Social Sciences and Humanities.

18

It should nevertheless be noted that the figures in Table 6 do not cover the whole of R and D expenditure on environment since they do not include industrial research on "clean technologies". It can be seen that countries' efforts in the environmental field remained more or less stable in terms of the percentage of total public R and D expenditure between 1975 and 1982 (table 4) except in Germany (where this effort was almost doubled) and Switzerland.

In any event, there is reason to ask what the future trend might be. If the present economic difficulties push environmental protection into the background, then R and D in this field could well stagnate or decrease. On the other hand, increasing interest in energy and raw material conservation implies a significant development of "clean technologies" which generally prove effective in these areas. In addition, several countries (in particular France and the Netherlands) have introduced programmes to stimulate research into clean technologies. In this respect an increase in R and D related to environmental protection can be expected.

R-D in the field of clean technologies could well expand in the future.

If the concept of environment is broadened to encompass "Quality of life" (by adding R and D expenditures for "Urban on rural planning" to environmental R and D, in 1/10 000 of GDP - see Table 5) a decreasing trend can be clearly seen between 1976 and 1982 in most countries; there is however stabilisation in Japan and Sweden and an increase in France and Italy.

b)   Technical training

Technological innovation is rarely the result of a discovery made by a more or less self-taught isolated individual. It generally stems from an R and D programme carried out by a team of specialists. This "professional" nature of R and D and innovation is, according to C. Freeman (14), an essential feature of present technical change. Thus the training structures for researchers and technicians, universities, public and private research institutes, etc. represent the essential basis for technical change. While the purpose of the university system is not to innovate but to educate, it is recognised that technical change is facilitated by an appropriate technical training at the universities. The organisation of appropriate links between university and industry is also an important factor in technical change (13).

Technical training in universities is the essential basis for technical change.

Graph 2

Figure 53: **GOVERNMENT EXPENDITURE ON ENVIRONMENTAL RESEARCH AND DEVELOPMENT,** selected countries, 1975-1983

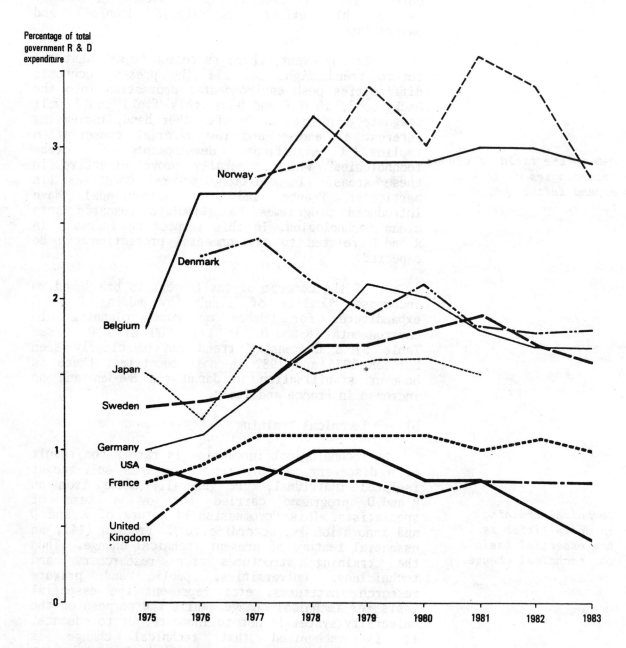

Note : These expenditures refer to R & D expenditures on pollution abatement, but do not include expenditures concerning pollution abatement throught changes in production processes themselves.

Source : OECD.

Table 4

PUBLIC R & D FINANCING FOR ENVIRONMENT PROTECTION (a)

Million US$ at 1975 prices and exchange rates as a percentage of total R & D expenditure (b)

	1975 $	1975 %	1979 $	1979 %	1980 $	1980 %	1981 $	1981 %	1982 $	1982 %	1983 $	1983 %	1984(c) $	1984(c) %
FEDERAL REPUBLIC OF GERMANY	42.5	1.0	93.6	2.1	92.6	2.0	84.0	1.8	84.0	1.7	81.7	1.7	..	..
AUSTRALIA	..	..	21.2	3.1	22.3	3.1	25.7	3.4	29.8	3.9	..	..	..	..
BELGIUM	6.9	1.8	10.2	2.9	10.7	2.9	11.5	3.0	11.8	3.0	10.6	2.9	..	..
CANADA	56.1	5.4	11.4	1.1	15.3	1.5	13.4	1.2	14.5	1.3	14.2	1.1	..	..
DENMARK	4.0	2.3	3.4	1.9	3.4	2.1	3.2	1.8	3.1	1.8	3.1	1.8	..	..
SPAIN d)	0.1	0.1	0.9	0.4	5.1	2.7	..	..	..	..	..	..	..	..
UNITED STATES	163.0	0.9	216.2	1.0	167.0	0.8	173.4	0.8	133.3	0.6	119.9	0.4	122.5	0.5
FINLAND	1.7	1.2	1.4	0.9	1.5	0.8	1.6	0.9	1.7	0.9	2.0	1.0	1.9	0.9
FRANCE	28.6	0.8	42.1	1.1	42.5	1.1	46.9	1.0	50.5	1.1	49.7	1.0	..	..
GREECE	..	..	0.7	1.2	0.8	1.4	0.8	1.3	1.4	2.2	..	..	..	..
ITALY	4.8	0.6	12.4	1.1	12.7	1.0	33.2	1.8	52.6	2.8	40.4	2.1	..	..
IRELAND	1.3	3.1	0.3	0.5	0.3	0.6	0.2	0.4	0.4	0.7	0.4	0.8	..	..
ISLAND	..	..	..	..	..	..	..	..	..	..	0.007	0.1	0.010	0.1
JAPAN	43.6	1.5	57.5	1.6	60.1	1.6	59.2	1.5	..	..	..	..	..	..
NORWAY e)	6.4	2.8	8.9	3.4	7.4	3.0	8.4	3.6	8.5	3.4	6.9	2.8	..	..
NETHERLANDS	..	..	..	..	..	..	..	..	..	..	22.3	2.8	24.5	3.1
PORTUGAL d)	1.0	2.3	..	..	..	..	..	..	..	..	..	..	..	..
SWEDEN	8.2	1.3	12.6	1.7	13.0	1.8	13.6	1.9	13.8	1.7	13.7	1.6	..	..
SWITZERLAND	3.8	2.8	5.8	3.4	..	..	4.0	2.7	..	..	..	..	..	..
UNITED KINGDOM	20.1	0.5	33.2	0.8	27.8	0.7	33.4	0.8	32.0	0.8	33.0	0.8	..	..

Source : OECD

a. Environmental protection includes R&D intended to protect the physical environment from degradation. It includes all research relating to pollution : study of origins and causes, diffusion and transformation and the effects on man and the environment. It includes research on "end-of-line" pollution controls but excludes research on changes in the production processes (the development of clean technologies) that result in the generation of less pollution. This research was assigned to the relevant category (for example, industry, energy, etc.), relating to the activities causing the pollution.

b. The GDP price index is generally used as a deflator except in certain countries where expected inflation rates are calculated by individual countries in preparing their annual budgets.

c. Forecast or provisional estimate.

d. 1975 figures refer to 1976

e. 1975 figures refer to 1977.

Table 5

PUBLIC R.D. EXPENDITURES FOR QUALITY OF LIFE (1) - 1976 - 1983 in 1/10,000 of G.D.P.

		1976	1977	1978	1979	1980	1981	1982	1983
GERMANY									
Urban and rural planning	(2)	1.4	1.4	1.8	1.8	1.7	2.1	-	-
Environment	(3)	1.3	1.5	1.8	2.3	2.3	2.1	-	-
Quality of life	(4)	2.7	2.9	3.6	3.1	4.0	2.2	-	-
CANADA									
Urban and rural planning		0.5	0.3	0.2	0.2	0.2	0.2	-	-
Environment		0.8	0.8	0.9	0.7	0.6	0.6	-	-
Quality of life		1.3	1.1.	1.1	0.9	0.8	0.8	-	-
UNITED STATES									
Urban and rural planning		0.6	0.5	0.4	0.5	0.5	0.4	0.2	0.1
Environment		1.0	1.0	1.2	1.2	0.9	0.9	0.8	0.5
Quality of life		1.6	1.5.	1.6	1.7	1.4	1.3	1.0	0.6
FRANCE									
Urban and rural planning		1.6	1.6	1.5	1.5	1.5	1.7	1.9	-
Environment		1.0	1.1	1.1	1.2	1.2	1.4	1.5	-
Quality of life		1.6	2.7	2.6	2.7	2.7	3.1	3.4	-
ITALY									
Urban and rural planning		0.3	0.4	0.4	0.5	0.4	0.3	-	-
Environment		0.3	0.3	0.4	0.4	0.4	1.1	-	-
Quality of life		0.6	0.7	0.8	0.9	0.8	1.4	-	-
JAPAN									
Urban and rural planning		0.6	0.6	0.7	0.6	0.6	-	-	-
Environment		0.6	0.8	0.8	0.9	0.9	-	-	-
Quality of life		1.2	1.4	1.5	1.5	1.5	-	-	-
NORWAY									
Urban and rural planning		-	0.6	0.6	0.6	0.6	0.6	0.4	0.4
Environment		-	2.3	2.6	3.0	2.4	2.7	2.7	2.1
Quality of life		-	2.9	3.2	3.6	3.0	3.3	3.1	2.5
NETHERLANDS									
Urban and rural planning		4.2	4.6	4.7	5.5	3.4	3.4	3.4	3.3
Environment		-	-	-	-	-	-	-	-
Quality of life		-	-	-	-	-	-	-	-
UNITED KINGDOM									
Urban and rural planning		2.1	1.7	1.4	1.2	1.3	1.2	1.2	-
Environment		1.0	1.2	1.0	1.1	1.2	1.5	1.4	-
Quality of life		3.1	2.9	2.4	2.3	2.5	2.7	2.6	-
SWEDEN									
Urban and rural planning		-	2.5	2.2	2.2	2.3	2.2	2.2	-
Environment		-	1.8	2.1	2.0	2.0	2.1	2.2	-
Quality of life		-	4.3	4.3	4.2	4.3	4.3	4.4	-

Sources : OECD.

1. The term "Quality of life" is defined here in the restricted sense of planning and environment. A larger definition would encompass the improvement of public transport, social services and health ; however such a definition would be too remote from the concept of environment in the strict sense (e.g. better transport systems are not necessarily less polluting and less noisy).

2. R.D. concerning overall planning of urban and rural areas, a better habitat and the improvement of public services.

3. R.D. on pollution, its origins, its causes, and the pathways of its diverse effects on man and the environment.

4. = (2) + (3).

Now, it seems that university research is at present suffering a certain decline which may be one of the reasons for the slowdown in innovation (15).

Generally speaking, technical training creates conditions favourable both for the emergence of innovation and readiness on the part of society to accept it. As stated in the OECD report (1) "the innovation process is tied into a continuum of institutions, behaviour patterns and minds"; this brings us back to the idea of "technical culture" mentioned above.

c)   The diffusion of innovation

*An essential need - the
dissemination of
technical
information...*

No less important is the existence of machanisms by which technical information is disseminated. It is necessary not only for technical information, a source of innovation, to circulate and penetrate the different levels likely to be able to use it (research institutes, industry, etc.), but also for innovation proper to be diffused broadly through-out the economy. This is particularly important for small and medium firms which need easy access to technical information if they are to innovate (16).

It will be seen that in the case of the environment, the existence of such mechanisms is an essential factor for the promotion and diffusion of clean technologies, either through direct State intervention (e.g. the "Mission Technologies Propres" in the French Ministry of the Environment) or through the intermediary of specialist trade organisations (Centre technique du papier in France.)

*...which should be
facilitated by
specialised mechanisms
and institutions.*

This penetration of technical information needs to be facilitated both at national and international level; there is no such thing as "technical self-sufficiency". This international dissemination occurs both through private channels and through intergovernmental organisations. The preparation of a catalogue of clean technologies by the United Nations Economic Commission for Europe is a prime example of an international mechanism for the dissemination of technical information.

d)   Financing innovation

Obviously, technical change requires adequate financial support, which may be based on public or private funds.

The respective roles of the public and private sectors in R and D financing have been

*The State must
facilitate the
financing of
innovation...*

discussed above. There is a whole series of financial incentives which can be employed: low interest rates for innovatory projects, special loans, development aid, etc. A broad range of measures has been instituted in Members countries and their effective operation is crucial to the enhancement of innovation.

By definition, an innovatory project contains and element of risk and uncertainty and it is important that firms, in particular small and medium firms, which embark on such projects can have access to outside sources of finance. Now, there is at present a certain scarcity of risk capital, particularly in the banking system, where there is little inclination to finance innovations. Moreover, high interest rates and the many economic uncertainties constitute additional obstacles to innovation financing.

*...especially when
no immediate financial
benefits are foreseen,
as in the case of
environmental
protection.*

It is understandable that the problem may be particularly acute when, in the field of environment, there is in addition to the uncertainty inherent in any innovation, a strong suspicion of "non-profitability" (in traditional financial terms). The authorities play a far from negligible role in the provision of risk capital, for example through giving guarantees to lenders or by creating public risk capital institutions which offer various forms of loan, such as loans convertible into shares, or which take an equity holding as in the case of the "National Research and Development Corporation" in the United Kingdom.

II. OBSTACLES TO TECHNICAL CHANGE

2.1. Diverse and numerous obstacles

This brief survey of the role of technical change in the economy and of its principal determinants gives some understanding both of the place of innovation and the relative importance of the different factors which aid its development. A good "output" of innovations depends on the proper functioning of these mechanisms, while if they function badly this constitutes so many obstacles. If the innovation potential dries up as discussed above, technical change slows down.

There are thus many obstacles to innovation. Without trying to establish any ranking, we would note that the most frequently mentioned obstacles are: financing problems and the shortage of risk capital; technical assistance and information problems, i.e. the lack of appropriate technical information dissemination mechanisms; the frequently inappropriate technical and university training and inadequate vocational training within firms themselves; the management of public aids to R and D; patent regulations; the practices of government contracts, many of which "bask in a benevolent routine where competition no longer has any place" (17); an inappropriate or poorly applied tax system where provisions to encourage innovation remain a dead letter; finally, timorous insurance practice which refuses to cover certain risks inherent in inovation.

Regulation is but one of many obstacles to innovation.

Among the most frequently mentioned obstacles is what is considered excessive state intervention in economic and social life. In particular, regulations concerning the environment are frequently stressed.

2.2. State intervention challenged

2.2.1 A changing doctrine

While economic thought already has a long tradition of reflection on technical change, the analysis and even the doctrine of intervention by the authorities in economic and social life has an even longer history.

Government intervention, alternately praised and decried...

In the case of Europe, it is worth recalling by means of a brief historical summary that the financial and economic discipline imposed by the medieval Church were followed by periods of central direction such as the centralising and interfering "Colbertisme" of the 17th century in France followed again by the laissez-faire of the industrial revolution. In most cases, liberalism and socialism finally converged towards mixed economies in which government intervention increase, at first in response to basic social needs, then to handle the increasing complexity of economic life and control certain of its negative effects (such as pollution). From this point on, the government, which has to regulate economic life, protect the most disadvantaged social classes, ensure workers' safety, and manage public health and the environment, multiplies its laws, regulations and interventions. This government intervention has resulted in particular in a significant expansion of public expenditure in the OECD countries, rising from 28 per cent of GNP over the period 1955-57 to

...results in the multiplication of regulations and a sharp increase in public expenditure.

43.7 per cent in 1976-78 ; in certain countries the 50 per cent mark has been reached or passed (18).

During the period of rapid growth and relative economic prosperity, government intervention was scarcely challenged even though the liberal and interventionist schools of thought continued to clash within the restricted worlds of the universities and learned journals. When the energy crisis appeared in 1973-1974, followed by a world-wide economic recession, the scene changed radically. After the increased price of energy had initially been declared the principal cause of the economic crisis, a more thorough enquiry began into the various causes and mechanisms of the recession.

In periods of crisis, government intervention is challenged.

Among others, one cause mentioned is the excessive burden of public expenditure which "diverts" a substantial share of GNP away from the directly productive sector. At times, the very role of the interventionist welfare State is called into question (12). Other causes mentioned are a certain number of rigidities which reduce the efficiency of economic systems by restricting competition or obscuring its more beneficial effects. At the origin of these rigidities, some people see excessively numerous and burdensome regulations that reduce the productivity of the industrial sector which has to devote an increasing volume of resources to "non-productive" expenditure in order to comply with the regulations. High among the productive expenditure deferred or foregone is that allocated to technical change, whose crucial role, mentioned above, is highlighted more than ever. Thus excessive regulation is considered to dry up a vital source of economic expansion.

2.2.2. Regulation and innovation : an ambivalent relationship

Environmental protection regulations are particularly resented...

...though this is but one set of regulations among many.

It seems to be the areas where government intervention has appeared most recently or has expanded particularly rapidly which encounter the most opposition. This is the case with environmental protection which did not take on any political, social or economic importance until the 70s. It is therefore not so much the regulations relating to health or safety, of long standing, the symbol and incarnation of major social victories, as anti-pollution regulations which are put in the dock. This exaggerated "visibility" of environmental regulations must not be allowed to obscure the existence or role of many other regulations; we shall return to this point.

Table 6

PRICE AND PRODUCTION CHANGES IN THE INDUSTRIES
SUBJECT TO ENVIRONMENTAL AND HEALTH AND SAFETY REGULATION

PRICE CHANGES	1958-69	1969-73	1973-77
	Average annual rates of change (percent)		
Most Regulated (includes mining; construction; paper; chemicals; stone, clay and glass; and primary metals)	2.2	6.6	8.8
Unregulated Manufacturing (total manufacturing with the exception of the most regulated industries and automobile manufacturing)	1.3	2.8	7.8

PRODUCTION CHANGES	1958-69	1969-73	1973-77
Most Regulated	4.6	1.6	-0.7
Unregulated Manufacturing	5.4	2.7	0.6

Source : U.S. Chamber of Commerce, (1979 p.14).

27

It is also necessary to avoid over-generalising: the "anti-regulation" movement, though fairly widespread, varies in intensity and degree of success from one country to another. In the United States, business and industry are strongly opposed to regulations which they deem excessive in number and in burden. One of the reasons for this is probably that they proliferated in the United States at a particularly rapid rate, and certainly much more rapidly than in the European countries (19). In addition, people are less accustomed to State intervention in the United States than in Europe which has a long tradition of intervention, as mentioned above. The United States is actually one of the OECD countries with the lowest public expenditure share of GNP (34 per cent in 1978).

However, this opposition is strongest against regulations that directly interfere with economic life. This is why each major draft regulation must henceforth be accompanied by a cost benefit analysis and by alternative proposals likely to resolve the issue. In the field of environment, the United States EPA is trying to promote more flexible and economically efficient approaches such as marketable pollution rights ("Emission Trading Program").

According to a United States Chamber of Commerce study (20), the most-regulated industries suffered both a sharper increase in production costs and a slower rate of growth than non-regulated industries. Table 6 shows that the industries most affected by health, safety and environmental regulations registered higher price rises and lower growth rates than other industries. These differences are particularly marked for the period 1969-1973. There is, however, no proof that they are caused by the regulations, which in any case, cannot be the sole explanatory factor - a great number of short-term and structural variables are involved. Furthermore, the industries concerned are for the most part not technologically advanced, high-growth sectors. Finally, it should be noted that the most important environmental regulations in the United States (Clean Air Act 1970-1977, Clean Water Act 1977, Toxic Substances Control Act 1976) were introduced later than 1970, so that they can hardly have had any significant impact on the period concerned (1969-1973). Furthermore, the difference in price trends for the period 1973-1977 does not appear very significant (0.9 points).

Nevertheless, the study brings out rather well the industrialists' concern about regulation.

They plead strongly for "deregulation", a neologism which may have a multitude of meanings as will be seen below. This concern is not the same everywhere however. A recent study by the Economic Council of Canada (21) covering all types of regulation shows that, by and large, industry is less sensitive to the direct cost of regulation than to the way in which it is applied - the "red-tape" aspect (many forms to fill in, etc.) is particularly resented. In short, it is not so much a mattter of deregulating as making the mode of application more flexible and less burdensome. This conclusion applies in particular to regulations concerning the environment, as the Council States that the advantages derived or to be expected from environmental policies fully justify their continuation and even their reinforcement. If there is to be any reform, the Council recommends that it should be in the direction of greater flexibility in implementation, in particular through the use of economic incentives.

It may be less a matter of deregulating than of making the implementation of the regulations more flexible.

However, the relationship between regulation and technological innovation is not a one-way process, while regulation may hinder innovation, it may also stimulate it.

a) Is regulation a brake on innovation ?

It is intended to enumerate below the main mechanisms through which regulation is considered likely to hamper technological innovation. This list will serve as a reference basis for identifying and analysing the features of environmental policy which may affect innovation (Part II of the report). At this stage, therefore, it is a matter of establishing a conceptual framework. It is also necessary to bear in mind that in many cases the causal relationships mentioned are in practice difficult to establish and impossible to quantify.

Reduction in resources available for innovation

Regulation has a cost for industry, not only in terms of the expenditure necessary for compliance (safety devices, anti-pollution equipment, etc.), but also in terms of administrative expenditure (negotiation, compilation of records, etc.). Industry therefore complains that financial and staff resources are diverted from more "productive" employment within the firm. By and large, the fact that a firm's profitability may be reduced by the cost of these regulations is invoked as a possible brake on innovation because of the reduced resources available for technical change and the increased

Regulation, being costly, can reduce a firm's profitability and affect its propensity to innovate.

risk which innovation represents where profit margins are lower (22)

Unfortunately cost estimates of regulations are quite scarce. A few estimates made in the United States indicate that the total cost (i.e. administrative and compliance costs) of <u>all</u> regulations. (environment, health and safety etc.) reached about 5 per cent of GDP in 1980 (23). These figures however do not enable any conclusions to be drawn as to the effect on innovation, which depends on the extent to which costs are passed on (or not) in the price and the extent of the real or supposed diversion of funds normally allocated to innovation, other things being equal. In addition, these figures represent only the gross expenditure entailed by regulation, without taking into account the corresponding benefits.

Diversion of R and D resources

The cost of regulation may affect R-D expenditure.

The lower profit margins mentioned above may reduce the amount of resources allocated to R and D, but there may also be a redeployment within the R and D budget so that part of the research effort is directed towards developing processes or products in compliance with the regulations at the expense of R and D devoted to directly profitable innovation. The overall R and D effort in OECD countries has certainly been marking time since the early seventies (see para. 1.1(b)), but there is no proof that regulation is playing any role in this phenomenon.

The case of the reduction of R and D in the American chemical industry is often cited as being due, at least in part, to regulation. Recent OECD studies on the pharmaceutical and pesticides industries nevertheless show that while there has been a certain stagnation or even regression in some countries, this trend is to be explained mainly through <u>structural</u> factors peculiar to these industries (tendency to improve product quality rather than create new products, arrival of these industries at the adult phase where the form and rate of innovation changes (24). It is nonetheless true that a part of the R and D human and material resources necessarily have to be used to resolve the problems posed by regulation, but the impact on regulation is not necessarily negative, it may be positive or neutral (see below).

Increased risk associated with innovation

Regulation may increase uncertainty and risk for the firm.

Regulation is frequently considered to be a factor aggravating the uncertainty and vulnerability of industry so that innovation becomes a more risky undertaking. This is considered to be due to the uncertainty inherent in certain regulations - uncertainty with regard to the content when they are being drawn up, then with regard to the date, transition periods, and modes of implementation. While it is true that in certain countries and for certain industries, the regulatory process has been subject to certain harmful erratic movements, this state of affairs should remain exceptional. The fact is that well-designed regulation should reduce uncertainty by eliminating ambiguities and unknowns. In addition, as noted by Hill and Utterback (22), the very absence of regulation can increase uncertainty by leaving the rules of the game undefined.

Another risk factor is related to the time limits and delays imposed by regulation, in particular with regard to the marketing of new products. For example, the delay in approving new products involves uncertainty and risk (in the case of chemical products).

Finally, the regulatory process frequently involves communicating confidential industrial information on the products or processes concerned to the authorities. Industry sees this as a risk which can be eliminated only by procedures which fully guarantee respect of the confidential nature of the information supplied. The establishment of such guarantees at the international level is in fact one of the objectives of the OECD programme on chemical products.

Inconsistency and rigidity in the regulations must above all be avoided.

It seems in fact that it is not so much the regulations themselves as the way in which they are implemented which tends to aggravate or reduce the degree of risk and uncertainty. Thus a survey carried out by the Denver Research Institue (1976, cited by Rothwell and Zegveld - 13 -) on the impact on innovation of EPA'S regulations mentions, among others, the following factors :

-- lack of precision on the scope of the regulations;

-- delays in promulgation;

-- disagreement between industry and administration on the significance and field of application;

-- contradictions in the varying implementation of regulations over time and between different agencies;

-- contradictions between the different regulations;

-- lack of information and explanation on the part of the regulatory authorities.

The study by the Economic Council of Canada (21), already mentioned, also emphasizes the role of the way in which regulations are implemented.

Modification of market structure.

It has been pointed out that regulation weighs relatively more heavily on small and medium than on large firms, so that some of the former may be forced out of the market to the advantage of the biggest firms. The innovation potential is therefore thought to be modified both by a decrease in the absolute number of firms capable of innovation and through a change in the relative share of small and medium firms in the innovation potential.

Does regulation particularly affect small and medium firms ?

The important thing is to know whether smaller or larger firms are the most innovative and there is certainly no generally valid answer to this question. While it is recognised that small and medium firms play an important role in innovation (12), the large firm is also considered a major source of innovation and the only one capable of coping with present technological complexity (14). Many studies have been made on this point (16) and the conclusion emerges that the contribution of small and medium firms varies according to country, period, sector and type of innovation (radical break-through, major technological change, simple improvement or imitation).

Size does not explain everything: each branch of industry has a specific behaviour pattern with respect to innovation.

The impact of modifications in market structures on innovation is therefore specific to each type of industry. Thus, in the chemical industry, firms with less than one hundred employees are by far the most numerous (83 per cent in Austria, over 50 per cent in Germany, 77 per cent in Switzerland, 87 per cent in the United States), which is far from meaning that they dominate the market, however (25). This structure nevertheless varies according to branch of industry. For example, the study of innovation in the pharmaceutical industry (25) shows that while R and D activities in this sector are largely dominated by big firms, the role of small and medium firms has only diminished slightly in the United States (26). The pesticide industry is particularly concentrated. In 1978 the 12 biggest multinationals accounted for over 75 per cent of world production and developed 57 per cent of new products, the remainder of the new pesticides being launched on the market by the 20 other firms.

The mechanisms discussed above concern the impact of regulation of all sorts on innovation - more specific to the environment are the following mechanisms:

Brake on the creation of new firms in polluted areas.

A brake on innovation or simply a land use problem ?

In a heavily polluted area, the establishment of new sources of pollution may be either prohibited or subject to draconian conditions, enough to discourage any new establishments. In this way, the innovation potential which a new firm would represent cannot materialise. It may be noted that the firm in question may try to establish itself in a more favourable location, which is obviously the desired objective, though there is always a risk of its escaping to a "polluters' paradise" overseas. One solution to this problem may be to set up a system of marketable pollution rights through which it might be hoped that innovatory reactions on the part of the firms concerned would be stimulated (27). Nevertheless, protection of polluted areas is not the only policy alternative - certain countries or regions may practise the "black spot" policy, consisting of "parking" the maximum of polluting industries in a single area.

Stricter regulation for new firms than for old, established ones.

Tighter control for new firms may discourage technical change...

...or stimulate it.

Implementing an environmental policy entails a certain change in the operating conditions of many branches of industry, so that special arrangements are necessary in favour of existing firms. This is why a whole series of transitional measures are introduced to this end, notably in the case of the exceptions to the "polluter pays" principle. By contrast, regulatory measures are immediately and fully applicable to newly-created firms. Sometimes even more stringent measures are imposed on them in order to benefit from or to stimulate new technologies (this was the case in Japan in the early 70s). It may be asked whether, in certain cases, this increased severity does not discourage the creation of new firms (sources of innovation since they frequently belong to technically advanced sectors). However, the environmental constraint has to be particularly strong. It is very rare for environment to be a decisive factor in the location or creation of a firm.

b) Is regulation a source of innovation ?

Regulation, and in particular that concerning the environment, may stimulate innovation through direct or indirect, expected or unexpected mechanisms, by stimulating the appearance of an innovation which had not necessarily been considered originally.

Expected and unexpected : two forms of innovation.

New technological constraints frequently have indirect positive spinoffs.

All regulation imposes a constraint to which industry tries to react in the most efficient fashion, i.e. at the least cost. In many cases, the most economic solution is an innovatory one. In other words, "the expected" is that industry find an innovatory solution to the regulatory constraints. Regulation is thus a stimulus to this particular form of innovation.

Moreover, this effort to innovate may stimulate a whole series of peripheral innovations which would not have otherwise appeared - this is "the unexpected". Thus the anti-pollution constraint may bring about a reorganisation of production and the appearance of new processes requiring less energy and raw materials. The long list of "clean technologies" and the numerous innovations associated with them may be mentioned here. This topic has been sufficiently developed elsewhere not to need any further discussion here (28). Regulation is therefore a challenge which causes processes or projects to be re-examined and brings about a series of innovations which frequently go far beyond strict compliance with regulations.

Stimulation of R and D

New blood in R-D services.

The regulatory constraint may bring about substantial modifications in R and D services by increasing their staff and resources or through reorganisation. The need for new skills, the necessity for an interdisciplinary approach, and recourse to new sources of information are important factors likely to stimulate increased creativity. The result for the firm is a better long-term capacity for the development of innovations, not only in the anti-pollution field but also others.

Increased profitability

More profitable technology favours innovation.

It was pointed out above that if regulation entails a reduction in profit margins, then it may result in a reduction in the resources allocated to R and D as well as an increase in the risk inherent in innovation. The contrary may nevertheless be true - clean technologies may bring about increased profitability, freeing resources for R and D and reducing risk.

Creation of new markets

Opening new markets is the best stimulus to innovation.

An innovatory reaction to regulation may put the firm in an advantageous position and open up markets for the new process or improved product. The anti-pollution market is a prime example - it concerns both domestic markets and exports of equipment and know-how. In France, in 1979, over 13 per cent of the exports of engineering firms were connected with pollution control (29). This does not mean that all the equipment exported was of a new type, but there is definitely no better stimulus to innovation than the possibility of opening up new markets.

Regulation designed to stimulate innovation

Regulation can expressly stimulate innovation.

There are many ways in which the authorities can stimulate technological innovation, but one way is for the regulations to contain specific provisions to this end, such as financing R and D activities, delays for developing new processes, etc. In part II of this report an effort is made to determine to what extent environmental regulations include such provisions.

2.3. The environment and obstacles to innovation

a) The context

The relationship between environment and innovation cannot be assessed without reference to the economic and political context.

In the preceding sections, an attempt has been made to put the relationships between regulation and innovation in the present economic context on the one hand and in the general framework of economic and social processes determining technical change on the other. This enables an assessment at the same time of both the importance of the problem and the place of environmental regulations in this larger context. Establishing the situation in this way is the essential precondition for answering the two-fold question posed, i.e. (i) what are the specific mechanisms connecting environmental regulation and technological innovation and (ii) how can they be used or influenced so as to promote both environmental protection and innovation? Any attempt to answer these questions without taking into account the context defined above would be pointless.

This initial overall analysis reveals that we are faced with a series of interwoven problems which, starting from a very general problem, lead to a very specific question. This series may be summarised as follows.

Upstream, the productivity problem.

Since there is a close relationship between technical change and productivity, the problem of relations between environmental regulations and technical change has to be considered very much in the context of the fall in productivity registered by the majority of OECD countries. Nevertheless, technical change is but one of the factors affecting productivity and in the chain of cause and effect, regulation in its turn is but one of the factors influencing technical change. Finally, the environment is but one of many forms of regulation affecting industry. There are in fact various types of regulation: economic (price, competition, etc.) and welfare (health, safety, education, environment, etc.). At this stage it is necessary to analyse the specific nature of these regulations and the mechanisms through which they are formulated and implemented.

The environment is but one of many factors involved.

b)   The mechanisms

The fact that environmental regulation may hinder or, conversely, stimulate technological innovation should not either reflect or give rise to irreconcilable schools of thought. The fact is that the mechanisms involved are often complex, always subtle and may act simultaneously. In addition, the majority of these mechanisms could operate in two opposing directions. For example, regulation may be a multiplier or reducer of uncertainty depending upon the case; the firm's R and D effort may be hampered or stimulated, etc. Finally, environmental regulations may take many forms (emission standards, technological standards, charges, various forms of economic incentives and licences, etc.) and may apply to fields as different as water, air or noise and to very diverse activities.

It is necessary to analyse the specific mechanisms through which environmental regulations may affect innovation...

The influence of regulations on innovation varies according to these many different aspects so that it is necessary to identify and analyse the different characteristics of environmental policy

at the level the characteristics of the regulations...

likely to have a positive or negative influence on technological innovation.

Furthermore, various studies concerned with regulations tend to show that quite apart from the characteristics of the regulations, the way in which they are implemented can have an important influence on innovation. In order to be properly understood these methods of implementation need to be analysed and evaluated at the level of the industry concerned. For this reason, the following analysis is based both on a general study of environmental policies and case studies in some 20 industrial plants in various Member countries for which a detailed examination has been made of the impact of environmental regulations on innovation and also of the way in which these regulations are perceived by those affected.

...and their implementation.

If there is a problem, what are the possible answers? There is much talk of "deregulation", a term which may cover many practices: abolition of regulations, easing or reduction of their content, non-application, partial application or application through new procedures (for example economic incentives). On the basis of the two levels of analysis mentioned above (overall analysis of policies and industrial case studies), an effort will be made at the end to draw conclusions as a basis action regarding the characteristics and methods of implementation of environmental policies likely to stimulate technological innovation.

Conclusions as a basis for action need to be drawn.

Part Two

CHARACTERISTICS OF ENVIRONMENTAL POLICIES LIKELY TO AFFECT TECHNICAL CHANGE.

As we saw in Part One of this study, regulations may have a positive or negative impact on technical change. Environmental protection is therefore a special constraint on industry and the question is how and to what extent the specific nature of the regulations and the way they are enforced can affect technical change.

Draw the lessons from the study of policies and industries.

This analysis is based among other things on a study of environmental policy characteristics in a number of Member countries and on the investigations into ten industries in various countries (30). This twofold global and sectoral approach enables a number of insights to be drawn, in particular regarding the main factors likely to influence technical change. However, no firm conclusion can be drawn on the relative weight of these different factors, the study having necessarily covered a limited sample of countries and industries.

I.   THE RULE-MAKING PROCESS

1.1.   Involvement of industry in the rule-making process and relations between industry and government.

Need for balanced co-operation between industry and government...

Balanced co-operation between government and industry can facilitate technical progress since it permits an exchange of information on technical data and on ways and means of prompting the changes required. This increased realism is backed by greater familiarity with the regulations on the part of industry, which is in a better position to respond, especially if co-operation exists right from the start of the rule-making process. Indeed, the fact that industry can take account of environmental concerns at an early stage in its investment plans is very promising for technical change. At the same time, the involvement of industry considerably reduces the uncertainty concerning the scope, and duration of the regulations, and doubts as to when they are to be enforced, which could make technological change drag its heels (see below).

Of course, this co-operation must involve give and take : industry must not be allowed to get away with the fixing of lax standards nor must the government impose unrealistic ones (see Section 2.2).

Experience shows that co-operation can take several forms according to the countries or cases considered. Thus, industry-government relations can be institutionalised, or improvised case by case and may be formal or informal.

In several countries, special institutions and mechanisms have been set up for this purpose. In France, the "Conseil Supérieur des Installations Classées", which decides what kinds of establishment have to be licensed, includes representatives of industry, and it is not rare for negotiations at national level to take the form of contracts for a whole branch of industry. Similar mechanisms exist in several other countries. The industrial case studies tend to confirm the positive outcome of such co-operation.

For example, in Canada, a joint industry-government working group has determined the technical possibilities of reducing the effluent from the pulp and paper industry. In the Netherlands, the government has consulted the leather tanning industry on suitable standards and the technical means of promoting them, while the sugar industry has benefited from early action by the regulatory authorities, which have planned and negotiated the content and scope of the environmental regulations in advance. Norway and Sweden provide good examples of consultation between industry and government which has produced efficient technical solutions.

While it is generally useful, this co-operation between industry and government does not automatically produce the best results. In France, the "branch contract" signed with the pulp and paper industry has had varying results according to individual firms: the contract provided for an 80 per cent reduction in five years of the effluent from this industry; this has been fully complied with, but most firms have been content with traditional solutions (end-of-line treatment) and only a minority have attempted any innovation by modifying their production processes. This shows that a good many other factors govern firms'innovation policy (see below).

Advantages of co-operation in the field...

Another aspect of this co-operation is that it may be centralised or decentralised. The regulations may be prepared or enforced at regional or local level. Usually, national regulations are adapted and applied at decentralised State, regional or prefectural level, according to the case. At this level, consultation between government and industry can be particularly fruitful since it is nearer "the field" and in the actual theatre of operations. In the case of France, for example, the decentralised implementation of regulations (Comités et Agences de Bassin, Service des Mines) is a strong element of the technical co-operation between State and Industry; the study of the metal-plating industry shows that by supplying the necessary technical information, the regional authorities have helped to solve this industry's problems. What should be noted here is the need for links at a decentralised level for permanent technical co-operation between State and Industry.

...over conflictual relations.

Finally, the importance of the relations between government and the private sector should be noted. Whether they are co-operative or conflictual in character has a significant impact. In Sweden, for example, a hundred years old tradition of co-operation has made a considerable contribution to the solution of environmental problems (31). Most of the industrial case studies carried out in this review stress this aspect: in the United States, where government-industry relations are usually conflictual (regulations challenged in the courts), the EPA is endeavouring to introduce co-operation and consultation with industry(32).

The motor industry provides a contrasting example of these two types of relations: the United States experienced many years of conflict between government and car manufacturers which culminated in 1981 in the revocation of 34 safety and environmental standards revision or modification. On the other hand, quite broad consultation exists in Europe, both at national and international level (EEC).

Naturally, useful though it may be, consultation is not the universal answer and an even balance must be found between insufficient and excessive consideration of industry's point of view.

1.2. Duration of the rule-making process

Manage time so as to minimise uncertainty.

A sufficiently long rule-making process facilitates broader discussion with all the parties concerned and enables the regulatory authorities to solve any problems at the outset through regulations whose terms or operative dates will need no subsequent revision. This reduces uncertainty for firms. However, an excessively long rule-making period can delay the introduction of suitable technologies and, in certain cases, increase uncertainty in industry.

In most of the cases studied, the rule-making process appears to be quite slow and to take several years. But it is impossible to generalise as there are so many variations between countries and between regulations.

It cannot therefore be claimed that the duration of the rule-making process is in itself a factor likely to affect technical change. The important thing is how the time available is used: if it is part of a process of consultation with industry, it can be a positive factor; if it entails an erratic procedure involving projects, amendements and ajournements, industry can suffer. The leather industry in the Netherlands has suffered from the over hasty enforcement of the legislation on solid waste; but the sugar industry in the same country has had sufficient time to introduce the best possible methods. Governments should also take care not to publish decrees implementing legislation months or even years after promultation.

1.3. Co-ordination of government regulations

Constantly keep an overall view of the various technical requirements.

There can be no doubt that inconsistency between regulations and lack of co-ordination between responsible departments can prove a major obstacle to technical change. It is not uncommon for industry to be faced with contradictory technical requirements, such as to reduce energy consumption of cars by developing diesel engines while at the same time reducing noise emissions from these vehicles (the diesel engine being intrinsically noisier than the petrol engine), or to improve the structural safety (33) of cars (which means increased weight).

However, co-ordination does not necessarily mean dropping one regulation in favour of another: it would be a pity to sacrifice noise abatement and the structural safety of motor vehicles for the sake of energy conservation; the real aim should be to organise the response to any given technical challenge. Co-ordination means both organising R et D programmes to harmonize ostensibly contradictory objectives and phasing in the regulations concerned. Thus, co-ordination applies to the various areas covered by regulations (environment, health and safety, energy, etc.) and also to the different areas of environmental protection (air, water, waste, noise, etc.).

Co-ordinate the different regulations.

The issue is all the more delicate since problems are often complex ones identified only after the event when industry is already trapped in a technological impasse; this means backtracking, amending the regulations or launching new programmes at the cost of delays and wasted resources. Co-ordination therefore demands a both global and farsighted capacity for grasping problems; it also means overcoming long-established administrative divisions and inflexibility, and even reviewing the need for them. Not only must suitable mechanisms (interministerial committees, consultation procedures, etc.) be set up, but mental habits also must be altered; this is perhaps one of the components of the "technological culture" mentioned in Part One.

Some countries apparently already have co-ordinating mechanisms (though there is no means of judging their real efficiency), while others are thinking about setting them up. This problem is nonetheless often mentioned by industry as a major obstacle to technical change. For instance, the absence of co-ordination between the regulations on water and solid waste has been a considerable nuisance to the Dutch leather tanning industry. At the same time, the economic recovery programme of the Canadian pulp and paper industry was closely co-ordinated with the demands of environmental protection (34).

1.4.   International harmonization and co-operation.

Environmental policies are subject in varying degrees to international harmonization and co-operation. The objectives and scope of this international co-operation differ considerably: they may be strictly commercial (to eliminate barriers to trade) or ecological (to improve environmental conservation through co-operative research programmes and common principles of action) or else combine these two concerns. The scope of co-operation may vary: agreements on general

International harmonization has many objectives.

principles (such as the OECD and European Communities, Polluter-Pays Principle), programmes in specific fields (like the OECD programme on chemicals), bilateral agreements (e.g. on transfrontier pollution) or more integrated policies (e.g. the European Communities'activities).

Apart from specific R and D programmes designed to promote technical progress at international level, international harmonization and co-operation have other aims and a different rationale. Hence their possible impact is not easy to assess and would certainly vary according to the type of international action considered. Clearly, the greater the technological dimension of international harmonization, the more likely it is to have a positive or negative impact on technical change.

Avoid the pull towards the lowest common denominator...

Quite often, agreements establising common international standards and specifications aim essentially to remove non-tariff barriers to trade. The standards adopted therefore usually fall into line with established technological requirements that all parties are able to follow. This tendency towards "least common denominator" types of agreement is not conducive to technical change. European noise emission limits of 1981 on cars are a case in point: they are based on existing technology and were already complied with by about 80 per cent of all cars before the standards were ever introduced. Common product standards and specifications may also have the effect of reducing competition between manufacturers as regards the environmental (and other) characteristics of their products. Finally, international harmonization is often a tediously complicated process: it takes a long time to produce an agreement and a long time will elapse before it is revised (made more stringent, for example), if ever. Such international harmonization is less than likely to generate new technologies. International harmonization of standards must also be prevented from becoming an innovation-inhibiting cause of <u>uncertainty</u> to industry. This applies particularly to big exporting industries: some car manufacturers complain of the complexity and inconsistency of the harmonization processes relating to noise and pollution standards at European level; when several standards are proposed by different countries, which are the ones that matter? Manufacturers want more continuity and above all a timetable for the introduction of regulations.

...a sporadic action, which is a source of uncertainty for industry.

However, these shortcomings can be avoided and certain other forms of international

*A common effort of
research and
provision of technical
information.*

harmonization and co-operation can <u>stimulate</u> <u>technical change</u> by contributing towards the development of new technologies and their diffusion in the various countries. Thus, the harmonization of environmental standards and procedures would enable exporting (multinational) companies to combine their R and D efforts to develop technologies to achieve a common environmental conservation target. International co-operation could and should boost common R and D programmes, as is the case for the OECD programme on chemicals; the fact of no longer duplicating the same tests on the same product could release R and D ressources for the development of compliance and general business technologies. Furthermore, a "leading" country in a given technological area can persuade its partners to adopt standards and regulations based on this new technology, thus forcing some technical progress on other countries and minimising the risk of least-common-denominator. Finally, the very process of international harmonization can prompt specific kinds of scientific and technical progress: e.g. development of common testing and measurement procedures and promulgation of more stringent standards and regulations likely to stimulate technological change.

Generally speaking, it would appear that international harmonization should mainly affect products and countries which subscribe to specific agreements or are members of regional organisations like the European Communities. International co-operation could also lead to the wider dissemination of new processes. For example, the Economic Commission for Europe (UN) has launched a programme for the assessment and publication of information on the latest developments in clean technologies.

II. MAIN COMPONENTS OF ENVIRONMENTAL POLICIES LIKELY TO AFFECT TECHNICAL CHANGE

2.1. The instruments used.

Environmental policies are based in particular on a variety of enforcement, regulatory and economic instruments. Most Member countries use a combination of these instruments, although in specific areas policy may lean more heavily on one or another category.

a) Standards

Technical change may be promoted to a greater or lesser extent by the policy adopted, while the standards laid down, in the regulations can vary in their degree of technical detail (see Section 2.2 below). Regulation enforcement can also be adapted to back up the search for new technical solutions. Thus, in the United States, the "bubble" concept consists in imposing a general pollutant emission limit on a plant or a number of neighbouring plants rather than separately regulating each source of pollution in the same industrial complex. It is hoped that this will make it easier for the firm to introduce technical changes where they are most effective. The aim is in fact to allow industry maximum latitude in choosing a technical solution. The United States Environmental Protection Agency prefers this approach as a counterweight to the excessive rigidity entailed by imposing standards which tend to paralyse technical change.

Allow industry sufficient latitude in its technological choice.

b) Pollution charges

Among the array of economic instruments, pollution charges seem particularly appropriate for prompting technical change. First, a pollution charge leaves the polluter complete technical and economic freedom. Second, since the charge is proportional to the pollution emission, it is a permanent inducement for further abatement in order to reduce the amount paid and is hence a continuous incentive for finding more efficient technologies. Of course, the emission standards also induces the polluter to reduce his emissions at least cost, but without going beyond the limits imposed. The fact that the polluter has to pay for residual pollution is an additional incentive for reducing this cost (35). In other words, the saving made from a technological advance is greater in the case of charges than in the case of the emission standard; consequently, the charge is a twofold incentive for innovation: first, to reduce the cost of anti-pollution measures and, second, to reduce the amount of this charge.

Pollution charges, a twofold incentive for technological change.

The case study of a sugar refinery in the Netherlands shows that if efficient pollution abatement measures had not been taken, the charge paid by the refinery would have amounted in 1980 to 14 per cent of its turnover instead of the 0.14 per cent actually paid; this factor was most instrumental in accelerating technical change in the refinery; In the same country too, pollution charges account for 5 per cent of the leather tanning industry's turnover. In France, the charges paid by the pulp mills studied were equivalent to 1 to 2 per cent of their turnover during the period 1974-1978. Even though it is difficult to determine the exact contribution of these charges to technical change, their incentive impact can hardly be doubted.

This being so, the incentive impact of pollution charges depends on many factors, the main ones probably being as follows (36) :

The rate of charge should be neither too low nor too high.

Firstly, the amount of charge is a key factor; if it is too low, it will have little incentive effect ; if it is too high, it may result in a wastage of ressources. In France, as a general rule, the rates of water pollution charges levied by the Agences Financières de Bassin are probably not high enough. On the other hand, these rates are much higher in the Netherlands (five to ten times higher, according to the case.

Avoid erratic variations in charges.

Secondly, in the absence of adequate information on the various polluters' treatment costs, there is some uncertainty concerning the result which may be expected from a given rate of charge. This uncertainty must not give rise to successive government adjustments of the charges in order to "aim" them more accurately; that would lead to a very uncertain climate for industry regarding appropriate measures to take, which would be prejudicial to technical change. On the other hand, a timetable for alterations in rates covering a sufficiently long period would enable industry to take appropriate action in full knowledge of the facts, as demonstrated by the case of the sugar industry in the Netherlands.

Thirdly, the use made of the funds collected from the charges can stimulate or inhibit technical change. This would be the case if all or part of the funds were allotted to R and D on new production processes or treatment methods. In all cases where charges are levied in various areas (water or waste management, noise abatement), the funds collected are earmarked for pollution control. There can be no doubt that the criteria for their allocation have some effect on technical change (for example, assistance may first be given to industries which modify their production processes).

2.2. References to technology in the regulations.

Environmental regulations, and especially the various standards they include, are the outcome of all kinds of considerations and constraints: environmental quality objectives, political and economic constraints, and technical feasibility. Nonetheless, technological considerations are especially important, even though not exclusively so: to a large extent, economic and political "realism" stem from "technological realism".

Economic and regulatory realism are also the outcome of technological realism.

It is a fact that most legislation makes some sort of reference to technology, often using complicated and not always unambiguous terms: "The present state of technology", "The best available technology", "The best practicable means", etc. The meaning of these expressions varies according to country and from one case to another and detailed definitions are irrelevant here (37); but whatever terminology is used, the reference to technology may cover four types of attitude to technical change:

a)   The regulation may take the form of an "average standard", i.e. referring to a technology applied by most firms which can be easily adopted by others. This smacks of the "least common denominator" method. This practice, which is often justified on economic grounds ("economically feasible technology"), may have the disadvantage of paralysing technical progress, but the advantage of encouraging the wide dissemination of existing technologies. The cases of the sugar (United Kingdom) and metal-plating industries (France and the United Kingdom) seems to be based on this "average standard" procedure.

The environmental standard may reflect several degrees of technical requirement...

b)   The standard may be a "model standard" stemming from a technology applied by the most advanced and innovating firms. If nothing stands in the way, this innovation is disseminated and consequently has a beneficial effect on technical change.

c)   Taking the search for technical efficiency even further, we find what we might call an "experimental standard" for a technology developed in the laboratory or at the experiemental stage but which has not yet reached the industrial exploitation stage. In this case, more is demanded of the industry's innovative capacity (as in the Norwegian aluminium industry).

d)   Lastly, there is the "venture standard" determined by reference to very serious or urgent environmental needs for which there is as yet no technological solution. This is to some extent the approach used in Japan in the 1970s for air pollution or in the United States (especially in California) for motor vehicles.

But the standard is not enough on its own.

Obviously, these different approaches have very different implications for technical change. It is no less clear that references to technology, however stringent, cannot be absolute and must sometimes be backed up by e.g. R and D assistance, financial aids, provision of information, etc. (see below). In other words, the technological dimension of the regulations must necessarily be supported by accompanying measures; there can be no technological venture without economic realism. Similarly, technological stringency must be accompanied by a fairly flexible policy: a combination of technology-forcing standards and flexible enforcement can give the best results (sugar industry in the Netherlands, fertilizer, cement and aluminium industries in Norway, paper pulp in Canada).

Use performance standards rather than process standards.

Experience also seems to prove that there can be no technical progress without freedom of choice: the greater the regulatory pressure to impose a specific technology, the smaller the inclination to innovate. Thus, the process standard can force industry to take refuge in traditional techniques which are not necessarily the most efficient. On the other hand, the performance standard encourages the search for efficient solutions and even a complete overhaul of production processes. The technical successes of the Dutch sugar industry are due, at least in part, to its freedom of choice; in Norway, the practice of emission standards has also proved a factor for technical change; most of the industrial case studies demonstrate this point. However, freedom of choice does not mean laxity and the authorities have the difficult task of steering a course between this freedom of action and the demands of environmental conservation: there should be neither too much freedom without constraint nor too much constraint without freedom.

2.3.   Financial aid for pollution control

Usefulness of financial aid...

Part One stressed the importance of suitable mechanisms for financing innovation. Most countries have set up financial aid mechanisms for pollution control according to a wide variety of objectives and procedures (38). In view of this, financial aid for pollution control may be devised and applied so as to encourage technical change, and the study of national environmental policies shows that special provisions exist to this end. Two categories of financial aid may be distinguished in this respect : direct aid for investment expenditure and anti-pollution operation and aid for R and D expenditure.

...provided that it does not encourage the use of inefficient technologies.

a)   <u>Direct aid for pollution control</u> (capital and operating expenditure) may be granted subject to conditions which encourage the introduction of innovatory technologies, giving preference notably to clean technologies over end-of-line treatment systems. This is the practice, for example, adopted by certain Agences Financières de Bassin in France and the Ministry of the Environment in Norway. For this form of aid to become a real stimulus for innovation, a delicate balance must be found between the technological preferences imposed or suggested by the authorities and the freedom of innovation that the aid recipient is allowed. In any event, the industrial case studies show that financial aid can very much affect the technological response of industry: in Norway, financial aid for the paper pulp industry has been devised so as to encourage new production processes and the reorganisation of this industry. On the other hand, in Germany, aid for the metal-plating industry also led to traditional add-on technical solutions.

Locomotive effect of R-D aid...

b)   The government can introduce <u>special financial aid programmes for R and D</u> on new processes or products either by funding research bodies or by assisting given industrial projects. This aid may be granted on an ad hoc basis or through special agencies. In France, for instance, the Ministry of the Environments's "Mission Technologies Propres" (Clean Technologies Unit) distributes financial aid to industries for R and D in non-polluting, more efficient, and energy and raw-material-saving technologies; the Netherlands launched a special aid programme for clean technologies in 1975. The automobile industry also receives direct or indirect aid for R and D: In France and Germany, the government provides 50 per cent or more of the finance for large-scale research programmes on energy conservation and pollution control. Most of the industries studied which have developed new processes have received aid for R and D.

Government funding of R and D in new technologies can undoubtedly be used to stimulate

...provided it is administered so as to stimulate innovation.

technical change, but it must be efficiently administered and co-ordinated with other forms of financial assistance and the main components of environmental policy and adjusted to the specific characteristics and needs of the industries concerned (see below). An undifferentiated economic aid programme must not be allowed to blunt, not to say wipe out, the innovative propensity of an industry disinclined to get quick results from an R and D programme which is also subsidised but not related to other aid received. An error of co-ordination can slow down technical change: in France, the branch contract signed with the pulp and paper industry provided at one and the same time investment aid for short- and medium-term treatment targets and longer-term R and D aid for new production technologies. The result has been that a good many firms have resorted to traditional treatment without waiting for or trying to develop new technologies.

At the same time, development aid for R and D must be easily available and not hindered by too many administrative complications, a requirement which does not rule out surveillance of research by the financial backer to see that it produces results; the aid provided must be a kind of "aid for innovation" rather than an aid for R and D (13). Lastly, small and medium-sized firms, which represent a large innovation potential, must have access to the aid; yet, as a general rule, it is the largest firms which receive most government aid for R and D (39).

2.4   Government R and D activities

R and D is an essential factor of technical change and governments play an important role in this respect (see Part One).

In the environmental field, government financing of R and D is still at the very low level of 1 to 3 per cent, according to country, of total public-funded R and D (see Table 4).

Stimulus of government R-D co-ordinated with the private sector.

Nevertheless, this government financing of R and D plays an important incentive and locomotive role. In most countries, special government agencies conduct research on anti-pollution technologies, including the Warren Spring Laboratory and the Regional Water Authorities in the United Kingdom, the Council for Scientific and Industrial Research in Norway and the EPA in the United States.

It is not rare for R and D to be carried out by semi-public bodies financed jointly by government and industry. This is the case at the TNO in the Netherlands or the Water and Air Pollution Research Institute in Sweden. These joint institutions can be particularly useful to small and medium-sized firms, which can thus pool their efforts and reap the benefit of scientific and technical advice. In the Netherlands, the TNO carries out this function on behalf, among others, of the leather tanning industry, which consists essentially of small isolated units ill-equipped to respond to the demands of environmental conservation.

Lastly, the government can set up special R and D programmes, usually in association with the industries concerned, to help solve a particular technical problem (case of the cement industry in Norway).

As a general rule, the industrial case studies tend to demonstrate the importance of the locomotive effect of government R and D activity which, although it does not replace the private sector, gives it an impetus when necessary.

2.5   Government provision of technical information

Finance is not everything: adequate provision of technical information can be an important factor for the promotion of technical change. The government has an important role to play in this respect and public research bodies can and should be providers of information.

The government must make up for the lack of technical information for industry.

This necessity is increasingly recognised both at national and international level (see Part One) and most countries have taken steps in this direction or intend to do so. The industrial case studies confirm the usefulness of this provision of information. In France, for example, the provision of technical information has proved an important factor for technical change in the metal-plating industry; in Germany, the same industry has suffered from a lack of information. It should be noted, incidentally, that this function is not a government prerogative. The private sector has an important information function to perform through trade organisations (paper pulp industry in Canada, and in Scandanavia through the "Nordic R and D project").

2.6   Government procurement policies

Government purchasing power used as a stimulus to innovation.

The demand for new processes or products is a powerful means of stimulating innovation. As both consumer and investor, the State plays an important role in such varied fields as transport and telecommunications, health, education, defence, housing and town planning, etc. The economic "weight" of public expenditures is considerable and, in some OECD countries exceeds largely 50 per cent of GDP (see Table 7). Government procurement policy is therefore far from being neutral and can have a marked impact on innovation.

Governments are in any case fully aware of this and many of them deploy procurement policies which are intended to stimulate innovation(40). In the United States, the ETIP Programme (Experimental Technology Incentives Program) has explored many ways or organising public tenders and regulatory practices so as to stimulate innovation.

This potential role of the State can be all the greater when the public sector is at large. In some cases, the government even has a monopoly (defence, education, energy, space), not to say a monopsony as sole buyer of certain equipment. The closer the government is to a monopsony, the greater its power to orient and stimulate innovation through its procurement policy.

A large potential and a wide range of possibilities.

The size of the public sector varies considerably from one country to another, ranging from under 10 per cent of total investment to nearly half (see Table 8); room for action is nonetheless significant in every case.

As regards the environment, the government has a by no means negligible opportunity for action: municipal infrastructures (including pollution control measures), waste management, public transport, housing, etc.

In the field of pollution control, gross public expenditure accounts for 3 to 6 per cent of government final consumption (Table 9). But, apart from strictly anti-pollution expenditure, the government can ensure that its equipment incorporates non-polluting processes or products derived from new technologies (noiseless and non-polluting means of transport, clean technologies, etc.).

It may be the purpose of these procurement policies to disseminate innovation by providing new technologies with larger markets or to stimulate it by creating a demand for technologies which do not as yet exist or are in the R and D stage. In view of this, the existence of a market is a necessary but inadequate prerequisite for technical change. Procurement policies must be accompanied by other measures: guaranteed permanent markets so as to reduce uncertainty, an open door to other markets, a share for industry in the benefits of innovation (41).

Generally speaking, the management of public purchasing must be adjusted to these ends and stripped of the habits and rigidities which are as many obstacles to innovation (see Part One).

It should also be noted that the stimulation of innovation is only one of the objectives pursued by a government procurement policy which aims among other things to reduce government spending (42). Some objectives may prove contradictory and priorities must be established.

The study of national environmental policies appears to indicate that government procurement policies are still little used as an instrument for stimulating technical change in the environmental field. A possible approach therefore exists which is all the more promising in that it has potential and recognised effectiveness in other fields (see Rothwell and Zegveld - 13 -).

Table 7

PUBLIC EXPENDITURE AS A PERCENTAGE OF GDP
(1982)

Australia	31.1
Austria (1981)	44.0
Belgium	53.3
Canada	42.2
Denmark	56.7
Finland	37.3
France	47.5
Germany	44.8
Greece (1981)	-36.0
Ireland (1980)	48.3
Iceland (1980)	27.6
Italy	48.5
Japan (1981)	26.5
Luxembourg (1980)	47.5
Netherlands	58.3
New-Zealand	-
Norway	45.5
Portugal	33.2
Spain (1981)	30.3
Sweden (1981)	60.3
Switzerland (1981)	28.1
United Kingdom (1981)	44.6
United States (1981)	34.2

Source : OECD

Table 8

IMPORTANCE OF THE PUBLIC SECTOR IN CERTAIN
MEMBER COUNTRIES IN 1981

Country	Number of employees (1)	Investissements (2)
Denmark	3.6	-
Luxembourg	4.5	6.0
Netherlands	5.8	11.0
United-Kingdom	8.1	20.0
Greece	8.6	11.4
Ireland (1979)	9.0	12
Belgium	10.0	12
Germany	10.5	12.7
France (1982)	14.5	33.5
Italy (1978)	25.4	47.1

1.   As a percentage of the economically active population.

2.   As a percentage of total investment.

Source: European Communities (43) and Bizaguet (44).

Table 9

POLLUTION ABATEMENT AND CONTROL EXPENDITURE IN THE PUBLIC
SECTOR AS PERCENTAGE OF SELECTED EXPENDITURE
AGGREGATES - 1978.

Unit : per cent

	(1)	(2)	(3)	(4)
Denmark	.96	3.9	2.0	.45
France	.46	3.0	.91	.19
Germany	.53	4.4	2.1	.45
Greece	.12	.73	n.a.	n.a.
Netherlands	.58	3.2	.92	.19
Sweden	1.69	5.8	2.5	.47
Switzerland	1.03	4.9	2.4	.50
United Kingdom	.74	3.6	n.a.	n.a.
United States	.56	3.1	2.0	.36

Notes :

1. Total Gross Public Expenditure for Pollution Abatement Control/Gross Domestic Product (GDP).

2. Total Gross Public Expenditure for Pollution Abatement and Control/Government Final Consumption Expenditure.

3. Total Public Investment Expenditure for Pollution Abatement and Control/Gross Fixed Capital Formation.

4. Total Public Investment Expenditure for Pollution Abatement and Control/GDP.

5. n.a. = not available.

6. GDP Government Final Consumption Expenditure and Gross Fixed Capital Formations are taken from National Accounts of OECD countries, OECD, 1980. For their definitions, see the same document.

Source : OECD.

Part Three

INDUSTRY'S RESPONSE TO THE ENVIRONMENTAL REGULATIONS

Innovation is also determined by industries' characteristics.

While the characteristics of environmental policies are not unconnected (far from it) with tehnical change, neither are those of the firms subject to these policies. Many of a firms's internal characteristics, as well as its economic and technological environment, determine its attitude to technical change. We must therefore examine the main internal characteristics of the firm governing its attitude to technical change and analyse the interaction between the firm and its regulatory environment (45).

I.   CHARACTERISTICS OF THE FIRM AND TECHNICAL CHANGE

1.1.   Size and maturity of firm and industry.

The age and maturity of a firm can affect its ability to introduce technical changes. Some authors believe that the firm's innovative capacity varies according to its stage of development. Thus, Albernathy (46) and Utterback (47) have elaborated the theory of the firm's "life cycle".

In the first phase of this cycle, the firm is small and uses flexible production methods on a small highly labour-intense scale and is able to absorb basically new processes and products relatively easily.

During the second phase, the firm begins to increase its sales and its output of one or more products. To do this, it must find more efficient manufacturing methods. It therefore develops certain basically new processes (e.g. machanisation or automation of part of the production system). However, as output rises, production systems become more inflexible and technical changes consist of marginal improvements.

Are mature industries the most technologically inflexible ?

Finally, in the third phase, the firm concentrates on selling a standardized product for the lowest cost. It therefore develops highly integrated and very capital-intensive mass production methods using special equipment. The cost of making any fundamental change in its production methods is very high. It therefore makes only gradual changes in its products and processes in order to reduce its costs. In this last phase, the firm will probably be still larger and will have a more complex and more centralised management structure.

The study of the industries mentioned above only partly confirms these hypotheses. For instance, sugar refining in the United Kingdom is an old-established industry (all the firms date from before 1935) whose production process has remained unchanged in the face of environmental regulations which are, admittedly, technically undemanding. Similarly, the age of the leather tanning industry in the Netherlands has apparently put a brake on technical change for that industry, which has preferred "conventional" end-of-pipe treatment solutions to changing its production processes (48). Again, maturing industries such as paper pulp in France have shown some resistance to technical change and been content with end-of-pipe treatment processes.

...industries with most experience being often the most innovative...

However, many now mature large industries have demonstrated great innovative capacity, which proves that age and maturity are not necessarily a cause of inflexibility but may on the contrary be a source of experience and capability for technical change, as in the case of the fertilizer industry in Norway, sugar refining in the Netherlands or the paper pulp industry in Canada.

An important characteristic of the firm is its <u>size</u>. As stated in Part One (Section 2.3), while big firms are usually a major source of innovation, the role of the SMEs is far from being negligible and they represent an important innovation potential. It cannot necessarily be concluded therefore that small size is a handicap. However, among the industries studied, small firms have in most cases proved to be less open to technical change than big production units. The <u>structure</u> of the industry has a special influence. Indeed, when the industry is highly fragmented and contains many small units, it is harder and slower for technical change to penetrate: this is the case for the leather industry in the Netherlands and the metal-plating industry in France, the United Kingdom and Germany. First, the small size of firms prevents them from undertaking any large-scale R and D, and, secondly, the fragmented structure of the industry is a special hindrance to the

This has only proved true in certain cases...

...as well as large firms.

penetration and circulation of technical information to each firm.

Collective organisation of R and D and information channels therefore becomes necessary, as in the Dutch leather tanning industry (see Section 1.6). The government too has the task of assisting R and D and facilitating the penetration of technical change.

Technological dependances is a handicap.

As a general rule, small production units are technically dependent on outside sources: government aid, collective R and D institutes or purchase of equipment from specialised suppliers (e.g. purchase of pollution abatement equipment); in this latter case, pollution control tends to take the form of"add-on" systems rather than changes in production processes. When an industry consists both of SMEs and a few large highly innovative units, the SMEs remaining on the market can benefit to some extent from the locomotive effect of technical change in the big firms. Something of the sort has happened in the chemical industry (see Part One). In the case of the motor industry, "small" manufacturers such as Volvo and Saab have also been very innovative.

Big firms have easier access to technical information.

Finally, when an industry comprises only a few large units, its innovation potential is necessarily concentrated and rationalised. Take the special and perhaps extreme case of Norway, where the heavy concentration of the industries studied constitutes a powerful factor for technical change; this is true of the cement and fertilizer industries, each belonging to one company only, and of the aluminium industry, where a single firm is responsible for 45 per cent of this industry's output. In each case, intensive R and D activity, associated with advanced tehnological capability, has facilitated the introduction of innovative solutions for pollution control, as well as in other areas (energy and raw materials). In the Netherlands, the fact that two well-structured well organised groups share the sugar industry gives a strong impetus to technical change.

1.2. Economic position of the firm

The firm's <u>financial capacity</u>, together with the industry's present economic position and future outlook, can affect technical change.

A healthy financial capacity does of course facilitate technical change, even though it is not a decisive factor: an ample cash flow is only an operational instrument. It is in any case possible for an idyllic financial position to be detrimental to technical change in a firm which is resting on its laurels.

Cash flow is not the only element of financial capacity: access to external financial sources is essential. Investors must also be willing to finance R and D or investments in new technologies of uncertain profitability. Part One stressed the importance of the supply of "venture capital", in other words finance for innovation.

The economic outlook and present position of the firm and industry are also relevant, but there is not necessarily any straight-forward causality between a good economic position and fast technical change, nor between a poor economic position and slow technical change.

The environmental regulations have more chance of stimulating a technical innovation in a period of industrial investment.

A period of growth is most certainly likely to be propitious to technical change: the Norwegian aluminium industry has experienced sustained growth which has enabled it to build up a strong R and D potential and to respond more easily to the demands of environmental conservation. On the other hand, since 1980, a downturn has compromised further modernisation of the production tool. The same applies to the ferro-alloys firm in Norway: the coincidence of a phase of economic growth and plant modernisation considerably facilitated an innovating response to the pollution control regulations, which have been incorporated in an overall strategy of production process rationalisation. In point of fact, a good economic position is above all a stimulus for investment, so that technical changes associated with the environment get the benefit of an already existing investment programme. We would once again emphasize the usefulness here of incorporating environmental protection measures as early as possible in a current or planned investment programme; it saves time and money, as demonstrated notably by sugar refining in the Netherlands and the aluminium industry in Norway.

A poor economic position can slow down technical change...

At the same time, technical change can be slowed down in a period of economic recession or industrial decline. The poor economic position of the leather tanning and potato starch industries in the Netherlands has been a major obstacle to the introduction of technical changes for pollution control purposes; the same applies since 1980 to the metal-plating industry in the United Kingdom, which has generally retreated into installing end-of-line technologies instead of changes in production processes. This was also the case for the paper pulp industry in France. The government can then provide aid through economic recovery programmes, tying the granting of a subsidy to pollution abatement measures (case of paper pulp in Canada leather tanning and potato strach in the Netherlands). It is in any case possible that a tight economic position may oblige an industry to rationalise its production in order to reduce costs; necessity is a law unto itself, and technical change becomes more than ever an imperative in these circumstances. Thus, in France, over the period 1974-1977, the penetration of "clean technologies" was greatest in industries where there was a relative decline in investment (except agri-food) (49).

...or stimulate it.

1.3. The firm's innovative capacity

The firm's innovative capacity is of course the end-product of many inside and outside factors. As regards the firm's intrinsic characteristics, the factors mentioned above - size and maturity, financial capacity - excercise a special influence. There is also a series of technical factors peculiar to the firm which contribute towards its innovative capacity.

a) The firm's technical rigidity and flexibility.

A firm may have more or less room for introducing changes into its production process. A modernisation phase is conducive to technical change; on the other hand, the production tool may remain unchanged for a long time after a period of investment. Thus, Ashford and Heaton (50) distinguish between "fluid" firms and "rigid" firms. A "fluid" firm is one in which products and processes are constantly changing and improving. A "rigid" firm is one which has reached a stage where it products are standardised and its production methods are highly integrated and more specialised.

The environment stimulates innovation more readily in technologically "fluid" firms or those undergoing transformation.

Technical rigidity can have many causes and, as we have already seen, certain mature industries can suffer from a certain technical inflexibility ("life-cycle theory").

On the other hand, the industrial case studies clearly showed that firms undergoing transformation or actively engaging in continuing production process improvement are, almost by definition, open to technical change. The environmental regulations then fit into this process of technical change with very little difficulty: far from inhibiting innovation, the environment boosts it and tends to direct it towards a more intensive seach for energy and raw material conservation (51).

b) Technical information

Industrial firms have various levels of technological infra-structure and experience which determine their innovative capacity.

SMes often have a smaller technological capacity.

Some firms have an R and D department which establishes perpetual progress towards technical change. The case studies confirm that industries which have their own R and D activity are best equipped to respond to the technical demands of pollution control. These technical innovations are always part and parcel of a strategy of production process improvement. SMEs are usually less well equipped and, since they depend on outside sources, they have a greater tendency to make marginal changes in their production technology or to purchase "add-on" systems. They also lack information on already existing technologies (metal-plating in Germany and France).

It should also be remembered that the firm's internal organisation may be more or less capable of reacting to a technological challenge: centralised or decentralised decision-making, room for initiative, rigid decision-making processes, internal circulation of technical information and receptiveness to outside sources of information are all factors which affect technical change.

c) The firm's technological environment

Access to technical information is important.

The firm comes under the influence of its technological environment, which includes such factors as the industry's rate of technological development or the lead given by particularly innovative and productive firms. As a rule, technical change and expansion go hand in hand for an industry. Receptiveness to this environment is all-important: many cases show that those firms which are receptive to outside sources of technical information are precisely the ones which innovate. When communication is difficult, the government has the task of improving the penetration of technical information (see Part Two, section 2.5).

1.4 Collective organisation of R and D

Strength lies in unity; in business, it also permits economies of scale. Industry has not failed to apply this principle to R and D by setting up collective R and D structures, often in one and the same sector. We have already mentioned that this kind of organisation of R and D is particularly advantageous for SMEs.

As may be seen from Table 10, collective industrial research exists in many countries, although it accounts for only a small percentage of total industrial R and D (between 1 and 5 per cent, according to the country). The State usually helps to finance such centers, either by direct grants or through research contracts. Rothwell and Zegveld (13) note in this connection that the State fills an important role by orienting industrial research to public interest areas such as the environment and health. They suggest that the collective research institutes in these areas poll their resources in order to tackle certain specific problems instead of working separately; the State can act as a catalyst here, for example by setting up special R and D programmes.

In R-D, strength lies in unity.

The State can encourage collective R-D.

Collective R and D plays an important role in the environmental field either through existing organisations or through new special R and D institutes. In France, the "Centre Technique du Papier", funded by the pulp and paper industry, is conducting an R and D programme on "clean technologies", albeit at government prompting. In the Netherlands, we have already referred to the part played by the TNO in developing chromium recycling techniques for the leather tanning industry. The government has adopted the habit of signing research contracts with the TNO in special areas such as the environment. In Norway and Sweden, the paper pulp industry has pooled its resources for a large-scale R and D programme.

1.5 Markets for new processes and products

The opening of new markets is a powerful stimulus for innovation.

The prospect of introducing new processes or products to the market is a powerful stimulus for innovation. In the environmental field, industry can patent and sell pollution control processes or new non-polluting technologies on domestic and international markets. Thus, the innovating performance of the motor industry depends very much on home and foreign markets. Manufacturers may decide to bring their vehicles into line with the standards of other countries (or groups of countries) if their market is sufficiently large; this may lead to innovations on these vehicles. On the other hand, a market which is too small may incline the manufacturer to give it up rather than launch into the expensive modification of exported vehicles. This has happened for the Renault and Peugeot-Citröen groups, which have reduced the range of models exported to Switzerland because that country's noise emission limits are stricter than in the EEC. The Swedish regulations, which are similar to those in the United States, have led the nine major EEC manufacturers to offer only 135 models on that market, as against the 335 available on the Communities market.

However, in the case of the automobile industry, it must be noted that environmental considerations are less likely to be suported by the market. In fact, the more a regulation meets the needs actually felt by motor vehicle users, the more it is likely to create a demand which manufacturers will try to meet: lower energy consumption and more safety correspond to the wishes of users; but this is not the case for pollution and noise (outside the vehicle) which are considered in a less positive manner by manufacturers.

In Norway, the cement industry has developed a toxic waste incineration process with energy recovery which makes a 6 per cent saving on production costs. This process will be marketed. In the Netherlands, a sugar refinery has patented a water treatment process which is 90 per cent efficient and recovers methane gas. The earnings thus obtained cover a good part of the cost of developing this process.

Marketing innovation can also give them a wider circulation.

It should also be noted that this marketing of new technologies is an important means of diffusing technical change throughout the economy. At the same time, the marketing of the new products and processes initiated by pollution control would be facilitated by imporving the circulation of detailed information on these innovations and their uses. Embryo by product markets already exist in the form of "waste exchanges", some of which are profitable enough to attract private management. The market for pollution control equipment is also expanding with the growing number of exhibition fairs and special magazines. The incentive for technical change will be all the greater if it can rely on a well-informed efficient market.

Table 10

SUMMARY OF COLLECTIVE INDUSTRIAL RESEARCH EFFORT IN EIGHT COUNTRIES

Country	Collective research organizations	Manpower employed	Expenditure on collective research	Percentage of total industrial R & D expenditure	Source of funding
France	22 industrial technical centres	5239 (1976)	850 million francs (1976)	5	7% (1978) Public financing 59% parafiscal taxes and voluntary subscriptions 34% own resources (private contracts etc.)
Japan	18 government centres; 187 local centres	4115 (1976); 6115 (1976)	29 760 million yen; 31 000 million yen	1.0; 1.1	100% government funding; 90% local authority; 3-9% M.Y. 1-7% industrial services
	5 semi-public centres	262 (1976)	2765 million yen	0.1	50-90% direct or indirect subsidies Approx. 30% from testing and services. Less than 10% voluntary industry funds
Netherlands	TNO Organization for industrial Research	1700 (1978)	18.5 million dutch florins (1978)	Approx.5	33% government stimulation subsidy 67% industry contributions.
Republic of Ireland	IIRS and Agricultural institute	1240 (1979)	L 19 million	-	IIRS: 37% fee-paid consultancy 63% government grant Agric. inst.: 100% government grant.
Sweden	23 cooperative research institutes	-	L 14 million	-	50% government funding via STU 50% industry contributions
United Kingdom	42 research associations	4718 (in 37 RAs) (1975)	L 70 million (42 RAs)	3.2	33% subscription income 2.66% statutory levy 27.3% government funding 33% industry contracts and contributions 5.16% information services etc.
United States	100 cooperative research organizations	-	$ 125 million (1976)	Approx. 1% of industrial non-military R&D	20% government contracts 80% industry subscription and contracts
	4 proposed generic research centres	-	Initially $ 6-8 million		Initially mainly government funding reducing to 20 % after 5 years.
West Germany	63 collective research institutes	3500	277 million Deutschmarks	3%	75% membership fees 25% governmental support.

Source : Rothwell and Zegveld (13).

1.6. The firm's innovation strategy

The various characteristics of the firm described above largely help to define its innovation strategy. This can be either: a _passive strategy_, whereby the firm launches into an innovation as a reaction to changes in its external environment; an _active strategy,_ where the firm looks for new markets, products and technology; a _combative strategy_ in which the firm endeavours to develop new products and processes quickly and to keep its dominant position on the market thanks to its technological advantage; a _defensive strategy_, where the firm does not venture into the development of high-risk advanced technologies incorporating much research work but instead lays down a sound technology and R and D base in order to be in a position to reacts and adjust quickly to the innovations developed by its competitors; an _imitative strategy_ by a firm whose technology lags behind the leaders of innovation; or, lastly, a _traditional strategy_ by a firm which makes no fundamental change in its products or processes because there is no change in its external environment and markets and no competitive pressure to oblige or persuade it to make such a change.

The industrial case studies clearly show that the most innovative responses to the environmental regulations are made by firms with an "active" and "combative" strategy, comprising the following characteristics:

-- existence of a large-scale and/or growing R and D activity;

-- constant search for improved production processes comprising savings in labour, energy and raw materials;

-- existence of a marketing capacity for new processes and products;

-- efficient communication with sources of technical information outside the firm;

-- positive attitude towards the environmental regulations.

In these circumstances, the environmental restraint does not upset a firm's settled habits, nor oblige it to investigate unfamiliar areas or change processes regarded as satisfactory. The environment acts essentially as an accelerator and a catalyst: the necessity to reduce pollutant

For firms with a "combative" innovation strategy, the environment is an accelerator of technical change.

emissions speeds up the quest for savings in energy and raw materials and puts this in a cost-reduction perspective (52).

On the other hand, "passive" and "traditional" innovation strategies are adopted by firms at a relatively low technological level which rely on outside sources of technology. The environmental constraint disrupts their habits and challenges their established practice and, according to the case, this either leads to a reaction of rejection or radical changes.

II. THE FIRM'S RESPONSE TO THE REGULATIONS

Positive attitude or rejection of the regulations by the firm.

Whatever the characteristics of a regulation may be, its scope and effectiveness largely depend on the way it is enforced. This is the point where the regulations come into touch with industry; the reaction of industry largely depends on the nature of this interaction between government and governed. On the one side, we have the firm's attitude towards the regulations and, on the other, the flexible or strict enforcement of these regulations. The firm may be immediately hostile to the regulations and spend time and money in circumventing them or disputing them in the courts; or it may adopt a constructive attitude and invest in research and innovation rather than lawyers. The industrial case studies show that a positive attitude by the firm helps to solve technical problems efficiently; but what makes this reaction positive? The government-governed relationship is a mechanism comprising several partners; certain methods of enforcing the regulations can influence the technological reaction of the firm (see below).

2.1. Compliance with the regulations according to type of firm.

Differential treatment of new and old firms appears to have no decisive effect on innovation.

Even though the law is the same for everyone, considerations of effiency and equity may persuade the government to make adjustments according to the types or sectors of industry concerned. For instance, a distinction may be made between old and new firms, the former enjoying derogations, moratoriums or lower technical standards, while the latter, on the contrary, have to comply with special technical requirements. This practice is very widespread in most countries. It may well be asked whether this might not paralyse technical change in older protected industries reluctant to innovate. There is also probably a danger that fixing stricter standards for new plant or extensions to existing plant will discourage investment in new machinery, etc. This has not been the case, however, in some of the industries studied, and notably the aluminium industry in Norway: the stringency of the regulations is not in itself a handicap; what is more important is the flexibility of enforcement and the firm's innovative capacity. At the same time, it is not rare for older firms to be given financial aid, as opposed to new firms. The terms of this aid may provide an incentive for technical change or, on the contrary, restrain it.

However, neither the analysis of environmental policies nor the industrial case studies have fully proved the assumptions mentioned above.

2.2. Stringency and costs of complying with the regulations.

It has often been suggested that the cost of the regulations could have a negative impact on industry because resources are "diverted" away from "productive uses (see Part One). Thus, instead of investing in productive equipment or R and D programmes directly linked with profitability, the firm allocates part of its resources to pollution abatement. The opposite argument could also be made: the extra cost of pollution control obliges industry to make a further effort of rationalisation, thus stimulating innovation. Four remarks may be made in this regard on the basis of the available information:

The effect of the regulations varies according to the industry...

a) First, although the cost of environmental protection is small at macro-economic level and not more than 1 or 2 per cent of gross domestic product, and although pollution control investment by the private sector is scarcely more than 5 per cent of its total investment (except for certain years in Japan - see Table 11), the economic weight of the environment varies considerably from one industry to another (see Tables 12, 13, 14, 15). Certain industries, such as pulp and paper, iron and steel, petrochemicals or food, are more affected than others. There is thus no all-embracing answer to this problem even if there is an actual diversion of resources. While the costs of regulation affect innovation in one way or another, this will vary considerably according to the industry.

b)   The economic weight of the environment varies overtime: during periods of implementation of policies, industry must make a special investment effort which diminishes as the equipment is installed (see Tables 11, 12, 13). If there is any negative impact on innovation, it should be temporary. This also applies to the real or assumed diversion of R and D expenditure: some of the industries studied have had to make a significant R and D effort on pollution control, allotting 20 to 45 per cent of their R and D budget for this purpose; these resources could undoubtedly have been put to other uses. However, this effort is usually always limited in time and the "environment part" of the R and D budget subsequently falls back to a lower level.

A strict regulation can be a strong stimulus for innovation...

c)   It is generally agreed that the stricter the regulation, the higher the cost for industry, if only by virtue of the law of diminishing returns (rising marginal cost of treatment). The industrial case studies show that this general rule must be qualified: in many cases, it was observed that a strict regulation was a stimulus for innovation and gave rise to efficient technological solutions (especially as regards savings in energy and raw materials). Nonetheless, raising the standards would probably entail extra costs; but it is still a fact that strict regulations can be a strong stimulus for innovation . Furthermore, the analysis of German environmental policy indicates that the industries most affected by the environment (defined here as those for which the environment has a net cost) had a 1.6 per cent better labour productivity improvement than industries for which the environment provided a net profit (53). Even though this does not necessarily mean that the environment is a direct cause of this productivity improvement, at least it has not been any hindrance to it.

...providing they promote conditions conducive to technical change.

d)   Lastly, the cost of the regulations appears to have no decisive impact on innovation. The industrial case studies show that the forms of regulations enforcement are much more significant: stringency should not be synonymous with inflexibility; flexible enforcement of the regulations according to a time schedule and procedures negotiated between industry and government are largely responsible for the firm's technological reaction. For example, the imposition of very strict standards on the Norwegian fertilizer and ferro-alloys industries led to profitable innovations because of the way these regulations were enforced by the government.

Table 11

ANNUAL POLLUTIONS CONTROL INVESTMENT (PRIVATE SECTOR)
AS A PERCENTAGE OF TOTAL PRIVATE INVESTMENT (1974-1980)

	1974	1975	1976	1977	1978	1979	1980
Denmark	-	-	-	4.3	3.5	-	-
Finland	3.4	3.8	2.0	3.1	1.6(a)	-	-
France	-	1.37	—	—	2.4	-	-
Germany	-	4.6	4.3	4.0	3.7	-	-
Japan (b)	15.6	17.7	13.5	7.2	5.4	4.9	5.3
Netherlands	2.7	3.2	3.5	4.7	3.7	3.9	4.0
Norway	0.6	0.7	-	-	-	-	-
Sweden	1.2 ·	1.1	-		-	-2.2	-
United States	5.0	5.8	5.6	5.1	4.5	4.0	3.9

a.   Water only.

b.   Manufacturing.

Source: OECD.

Table 12

POLLUTION CONTROL INVESTMENT IN UNITED STATES INDUSTRY

As a percentage of total investment

	1974	1975	1976	1977	1978	1979	1980 estimate
ALL INDUSTRIES	5.0	5.8	5.6	5.1	4.5	4.0	3.9
Manufacturing	8.0	9.3	8.3	7.0	5.8	5.1	5.1
Durable goods	7.3	8.1	6.6	5.9	4.9	4.2	4.5
Primary metals	16.6	17.2	15.7	15.7	12.6	12.4	13.4
Blast furnaces, steelmaking	12.1	13.5	15.1	16.7	16.8	17.6	19.0
Non-ferrous metals	21.8	24.1	18.9	17.1	10.3	7.9	9.5
Electrical engineering	6.8	5.8	5.6	3.4	3.3	2.3	2.1
Engineering (except electrical)	1.8	1.8	1.6	1.8	1.7	1.1	1.0
Transport equipment	3.7	3.4	3.4	3.1	3.6	3.3	4.0
Motor vehicles	4.1	3.9	3.6	3.5	4.3	4.1	5.4
Aircraft	2.9	2.8	3.3	2.1	1.6	1.5	4.2
Stone, clay and glass	12.9	14.3	6.1	7.3	6.6	5.0	5.3
Other durables	4.5	5.3	3.9	3.6	2.7	2.2	2.3
Non-durable goods	8.7	10.3	9.6	8.0	6.7	5.9	5.1
Food (including beverages)	4.7	5.2	4.5	4.2	3.6	2.9	2.8
Textiles	3.3	4.6	4.4	3.8	2.8	3.0	3.0
Paper	19.3	16.8	14.4	13.8	7.1	6.1	5.0
Chemicals	8.3	10.9	11.4	10.2	7.6	5.2	5.2
Oil	10.1	11.8	10.9	8.2	8.3	8.9	8.1
Rubber	3.2	4.0	3.4	3.3	3.5	3.3	2.9
Other non durables	1.8	2.8	1.4	1.2	1.5	1.1	0.9
Other industries (non-manufacturing)	3.0	3.2	3.5	3.5	3.5	3.2	3.0
Mining	1.8	1.9	2.2	2.2	4.3	3.4	2.7
Railways	1.2	1.4	1.1	1.0	1.1	0.5	0.7
Air Transport	0.0	0.6	1.2	0.8	0.6	0.4	0.4
Other transport	2.3	1.4	1.1	1.0	1.0	0.8	1.2
Public utilities	7.9	8.4	9.1	8.8	8.6	8.3	7.9
Electricity	8.9	9.7	10.5	10.4	10.1	9.6	8.7
Gas and other	1.5	1.5	1.2	0.7	0.3	1.0	0.9
Communications Commerce, etc. Commerce, etc.	0.6	0.6	0.5	0.5	0.4	0.3	0.4

Source : CEQ, 9th annual report, 1978, p.422.

71

Table 13

POLLUTION CONTROL INVESTMENT IN JAPANESE INDUSTRY (1)

	Percentage of total investment							
	1973	1974	1975	1976	1977	1978	1979	1980 estimate
ALL INDUSTRIES	10.6	15.6	17.7	13.5	7.2	5.4	4.9	5.3
Iron and steel	17.3	18.6	18.4	21.1	11.5	10.9	11.5	4.9
Oil	18.5	32.6	41.7	31.4	5.9	4.5	4.8	7.7
Thermal power plant	26.4	44.7	47.1	44.0	35.1	28.0	22.1	32.0
Pulp and paper	22.1	22.8	22.7	17.6	9.1	6.8	5.8	3.6
Non-ferrous metals	8.4	12.1	15.7	15.0	18.2	4.8	3.6	2.7
Chemicals (except petrochemicals)	17.1	29.1	32.8	17.6	8.7	5.0	3.7	3.5
Engineering	4.0	5.5	5.2	3.5	2.5	2.2	1.9	1.6
Petrochemicals	15.7	18.9	18.4	13.8	9.9	7.2	3.2	2.8
Mining (except coal)	24.4	32.9	37.9	37.6	26.2	14.5	15.7	3.0
Textiles	10.1	13.7	20.4	7.4	4.0	2.4	4.9	2.2
Cement	11.2	17.4	15.0	12.2	11.4	15.8	14.8	10.2
Ceramics (except cement)	9.9	10.2	10.2	8.2	5.8	10.3	3.7	11.4
Gas	2.3	4.0	2.1	1.5	1.1	1.2	2.1	2.4
Coal	4.0	2.5	8.2	2.7	2.1	0.9	1.6	1.2
Other	8.6	9.4	9.1	4.9	3.7	1.8	1.0	1.6
Construction equipment	5.9	4.7	7.2	4.4	6.1	4.6	2.6	1.9
Electricity (except thermal power plant)	1.1	1.6	1.1	0.9	0.8	0.8	0.7	0.9

(1) Estimates based on industrial engineering studies.

Source : Japanese Ministry of Trade and Industry.

Table 14

INDUSTRIAL POLLUTION ABATEMENT COSTS IN GERMANY

Industry	Pollution control investment as a percentage of total investment expenditure 1971 - 1977
Raw materials and producer goods	11.3
Non-metallic ores	9.2
Steelmaking	10.7
Wire drawing and cold rolling mills	1.9
Steel and malleable iron smelting	8.5
Non-ferrous metals (including smelting)	8.4
Oil refining	19.9
Chemicals	11.1
Sawmills and wood preparation	5.0
Wood and wood-based products	2.4
Pulp and paper	9.6
Rubber and asbestos-making	1.9
Durable goods	1.8
Iron and steel products	0.5
Mechanical engineering	1.3
Office and data processing equipment	1.4
Motor vehicle industry	2.0
Shipbuilding	0.6
Aircraft construction	1.3
Electrical engineering	1.9
Precision instrument and optical industries, watch and clockmaking	1.3
Steel shaping	3.4
Steel and other metal sheet working	2.3
Consumer goods	2.0
Ceramics	3.0
Glass	1.7
Musical instruments and toys (including jewellery and sports equipment)	1.9
Paper and board products	1.5
Printing, etc.	1.7
Plastics products	3.4
Leather-making	3.6
Leather products	0.4
Footwear	0.3
Textiles	1.5
Clothing	0.4
Food and beverages	3.2
Total manufacturing	5.3

Table 15

POLLUTION CONTROL INVESTMENT AS A PERCENTAGE OF TOTAL INVESTMENT
(FRANCE)

Polluting industry	Water pollution control investment (1970-1979)		Total investment (1970-1979)	Pollution control investment as a percentage of total investment
	Frs.million 1979	%	Frs. million 1979	%
Chemicals	976	20,0	67 873	1.4
Paper pulp	630	12.9	8 755	10.4
Paper and board	276	5.6		
Mechanical, electrical and electronic engineering	543	11.2	223 755	0.2
Oil refining	290	5.9	29 581	1.0
Sugar refining	236	4.8	8 480	2.9
Dairy industries	224	4.6	14 762	1.6
Wine distilling	130	2.7	1 437	9.0
Starch products	116	2.4	1 821	6.4
Rolling mills, wire making, wire drawing and pickling	97	2.1	5.981	1.6
Total (10 industries)	3 680	70.1	362 445	1.0
Total (all industries)	4 829 (1)	100.0	1.083.002	(0.4)

(1) Frs. 4.888 million over the period 1969-1979.

Source : Trink, 1981.

74

On the other hand, the absence of consultation, and excessive rigidity, force industry to take refuge in traditional and unprofitable technological solutions.

This does not divert the financial factor of all influence: it was also observed that the prospect of having to pay high pollution charges is a strong incentive for industry to find efficient technological solutions, as happened in the case of water pollution in the Netherlands.

2.3 **Time schedule for the enforcement of environmental regulations.**

Industry may be given a varying length of time to comply with the regulations.

A rushed time schedule inhibits innovation.

Too short an interval can discourage R and D in new technologies and rush the firm into hasty solutions such as to buy already existing equipment which may be more or less efficient and more or less suitable for the particular circumstances. This is the case for the paper pulp industry in Canada and France, which did not have enough time to introduce the best technological solutions. However, the technology imperative is only one of the elements of the problem : rapid enforcement may be necessary in order to put a stop to environmental deterioration.

Give sufficient but predetermined time.

Sufficient time allows industry more latitude to develop innovating solutions; technological change takes time. This will in particular allow pollution control measures to be incorporated in the general plans for improving production processes. But if too much time is allowed, it can lead to a certain laxity and blunt the motivation for technical change. Industry may then withdraw into a wait-and-see attitude in the hope that new technologies will be developed by others, which could easily not happen at all in the absence of a real demand.

The regulation enforcement schedule may also vary in strictness. A certain flexiblity and adjustment to the special circumstances of each industry can pay in the long run. This flexibility has been an important contributory factor to the technological successes reported for the Norwegian industries in the case studies since it enable the technical changes required for pollution control to be harmonized with these industries' other R and D and investment programmes. It is better to have regulations that are strict but flexibly enforced, than undemanding regulations hastilly enforced.

2.4. Ease of obtaining exemptions

An exemption may consist in cancelling, relaxing or postponing the provisions of a regulation. As a rule, exemption weakens the regulations and can be prejudicial to technical change, not to speak of the negative consequences for the environment. Exemptions are current practice in most countries, usually for economic and social reasons, at regional and local level.

The possibility of obtaining an exemption must depend on the beneficiary's work specifications.

An exemption which allows industry sufficient time and latitude to develop new technologies is usually favourable for technological change. There may, however, be a conflict between the desire to facilitate technical change and the urgent need to protect the environment, which often means a conflict between urgent short-term measures and greater efficiency in the longer term.

In the United States, the Clean Water Act and the Air Pollution Act provide exemptions for industries which launch more efficient new technology development programmes. Krupnick and Yardas (54) consider, however, that these provisions have not been very effective. They report that by mid-1980 the EPA had received only 20 formal applications for exemption under the provisions of the Air Pollution Act, which came into force back in 1977. Admittedly, this Act's provisions have not been very widely publicised. Exemptions have apparently been granted a posteriori to a large number of firms which could not comply with the time-limits imposed for introducing measures to reduce water pollution. Granting exemptions a posteriori could quite invalidate innovation promotion measures, which must, on the contrary, provide beforehand for an R and D programme in new technologies. Exemptions should consist of a virtual "technological progress contract" between industry and government whereby industry undertakes to carry out a given programme in exchange for a moratorium. This smacks of the spirit of the "branch contracts" in vogue in France. It also has overtones of the Norwegian approach, which consists in combining stringent regulations with flexible enforcement procedures (sufficiently long grace period, free choice of technologies), providing flexibility does not mean laxity.

2.5. Uncertainty

Many analysers have noted that industry's uncertainty regarding its future and its economic

*Uncertainty, the
enemy of innovation...*

and regulatory environment could be prejudicial to technical change. Research and experiment in new technologies are already in themselves a hazardous venture and a maximum number of parameters must be provided and checked by industry.

Uncertainty may exist at several levels. First, there is technological uncertainty about the success or failure of the technical changes made. To this must be added financial uncertainty about the amount of future expenditure which the firm will have to commit to implement the innovation plan, as well as market uncertainty concerning the firm's ability to actually sell a new product or process. This also includes the risk that the benefits expected form the innovation may be tempered by changes in future economic conditions and by the technology advances of the firm's competitors.

This uncertainty may lead to wrong estimates or to negative effects due to unexpected events: in the Netherlands, the potato starch industry suffered from both effects: First, the technical changes introduced to comply with new stricter environmental regulations turned out to be more costly than initially forecast, in particular owing to energy prices; second, the sales of by-products (cattle food) were not profitable enough because prices were too low.

Lastly, regulatory uncertainty exists regarding various aspects of the regulations. This uncertainty may concern :

...may take many forms.

-- The time factor: time for enforcing the regulations not stated, excessive delay between promulgation of a law and its actual implementation (see above). Too frequent changes in the enforcement schedule (postponement of time-limits) are prejudicial to investment planning. The many mishaps arising under the regulations on the United States automobile industry are a case in point. Similarly, the procedure for increasing pollution charges must be worked out and published in advance so that industry can take appropriate action.

-- The content of the regulations: lack of precision in the regulations, especially as regards the government's "technological preferences", i.e. recommended treatment technologies. We have already stressed that the vagueness of certain references to "best technologies available" or "practicable" could be a source of uncertainty.

-- The continuity of the regulations, since too frequent amendments create a climate of uncertainty which is prejudicial to innovation.

The content of the regulations should be notified in advance.

Most Member countries have taken steps to avoid any regulatory uncertainty, especially by associating industry with the rule-making process and providing for sufficiently flexible enforcement.

This is confirmed by the industrial case studies. It will be noted, however, that the Netherlands leather-tanning industry hesitated to change its production processes because the legislation on toxic wastes was so long in the making and because of the initial absence of co-ordination between this and the water pollution legislation.

In the United States, the quite frequent changes made in the regulations and their dates of enforcement have created a prejudicial climate of uncertainty. In Europe, the motor vehicle industry complains of the uncertainty over the future regulations negotiated in Geneva (WP.29) and Brussels; some manufacturers would prefer standards that were stricter but were introduced according to a specific long-term schedule.

It should be easy to reduce or even eliminate uncertainty.

In any event, regulatory uncertainty should only be a temporary obstacle to innovation as it is largely linked with the transitional periods of environmental policy-making and policy enforcement. Moreover, uncertainty can be reduced or eliminated by a few simple devices such as information campaigns and by efficiency, clarity and planing.

2.6. Environmental protection specifications and the firm's flexibility.

The way emissions are measured can affect treatment technology.

The units used for measuring pollutant emissions can affect a firm's compliance with a regulation and its innovative capacity. Thus, if pollutants are only measured in terms of their concentration in the effluent (e.g. kgs of BOD per m3 of water), this may create a bias towards dilution or abatement technologies using more water. The regulations on the metal-plating industries in France and the United-Kingdom express the pollutant emission limits in terms of concentration and not the total quantity emitted; this may reduce the stringency of pollution control and hence the incentive for firms to adopt advanced water purification and recycling technologies.

What should be noted here is that the wording of the regulations can implicitly or explicitly bias technological change in one direction or another. The specification of pollution standards is not unconnected with technical change.

2.7. Interval between the application for and granting of a licence.

Too much time taken by the regulatory authorities to examine an application for a licence for a new plant or process can delay its construction or introduction and therefore postpone the commencement of production. In the case of licences for new products, a long examination period can delay their launching on the market and may also shorten the firm's period of patent protection for these products. Such delays could reduce the firm's future profits from technical change and discourage initiative in this direction; they might also dissuade an industry from incorporating environmental constraints at an early stage in its investment programmes.

Give industry time to allow for the regulations at an early stage in its investment.

As a general rule, excessive delays are a factor of uncertainty for the firm regarding the outcome of the administrative procedure. Industry has complained in some countries of procedures which are too slow.

2.8. Period of licences

The period for which is issued a licence can affect technological change in proportion to the degree of freedom the firm is allowed.

A licence issued for a long period is a factor of stability and reduces the uncertainty for a firm, which then has all the time it needs to plan an R and D programme on new technologies. However, if this period is too long, it can undermine and wipe out any incentive for further progress. Most countries issue licences for a fixed period of from 5 to 10 years. This period does not imply that the licence will be withdrawn on expiry but that its terms will be reviewed.

At the same time, if the period is too short, it does not give the firm enough time to make any fundamental change in its production processes and obliges it to buy an already existing control technology.

CONCLUSION: A TENTATIVE ASSESSMENT.

*Evaluate the importance
of the environment as
a technological factor
and government means
of action.*

In an economic situation when technological progress is more than ever regarded as a key factor of growth, the OECD Member countries have declared that it is necessary "to integrate policies for science and technology with other aspects of government policy" (55). The purpose of the present reseach, the main results of which have been described above, was to explore the nature of the raltionship between environmental policy and technological change in order to determine to what extent and throught what mechanisms environmental policy and the processes of technical change could converge or diverge, come into conflict or support each other.

In summing up, we might try to answer two questions: first, what is the real importance and scope of the relationship between environmental policy and technical change; and second, can environmental policy be so designed and enforced as to encourage technical progress?

I.   IMPORTANCE OF THE RELATIONSHIP BETWEEN ENVIRONMENTAL POLICY AND TECHNICAL CHANGE: A FIRST APPRAISAL.

I.   The context.

*Technical change,
a productivity actor.*

The problem of the relationship between the environment and technical change arises in a context of slower, not to say stagnating, economic growth. Faced with declining productivity growth during the last eight to ten years, Member country governments are now examining ways of reversing the trend. Although many factors are involved, it is agreed that technical change is a key factor for productivity growth (see Part One). Member countries have realised the implications since most of them now appreciate that priority must be given to stimulating technical change. Two types of measure are being employed for this purpose: first, the share of GDP accounted for by government expenditure on R and D (56) is being increased, or at least the falling R and D trend is being halted in certain countries, and, secondly, the obstacles to innovation are being removed and mechanisms introduced to stimulate it. In this general context, analysis of the relationship between the environment, technical change and productivity (see Part One) leads to the following observations :

a)   Many causes contribute to falling productivity, including rising energy prices, inflation and a complex "residual factor" mentioned in Part One of this report (see OECD, - 25 -, and Denison, - 2 -). While the environment's share in this process is still not clear, there is every reason to believe that it is relatively small, leaving aside the positive unquantified effects of environmental policies.

Many obstacles to innovation...

b)   If it is agreed, on the other hand, that technical change is an essential factor in productivity and if, dropping the macro-economic approach, we try to elucidate the mechanisms through which the environment can influence technical change (and hence productivity), we find that the environment is only a small cog in a complex machine and that there are many obstacles to innovation, including low R and D activity, unsuitable technical training, inadequate diffusion and financing of innovation, and a plethora of finicky regulations.

...including various government regulations...

c)   Lastly, if regulations are singled out among the obstacles to innovation, we cannot fail to see that those concerning the environment are only one category among many others (health, safety, worker protection, prices and competition, etc.) and that their macro-economic impact is in any event limited.

...and the environmental regulations among others.

Thus, in the context of policies for stimulating technical change, the environment is only one variable and in all probability limited in scope. But its small scope does not mean that it is unimportant. In view of the major stakes involved in technical change, everything must be done to accelerate it. The question is therefore, first, whether environmental policies are a real obstacle or on the contrary an encouragement to innovation and, secondly, how to go about making the environment not a hindrance but a stimulus for technical change.

1.2.   Pollution control as a technological phenomenon

a)   Magnitude of this phenomenon.

The environmental regulations oblige industry to take technical action to reduce their emissions to the level required. This action may take several specific forms:

-- installation of end-of-line ("add-on") treatment, with no change in production processes;

-- internal alterations enabling waste materials to be recovered and recycled, but with no change in the production process;

-- a major change in manufacturing processes.

Technical change may also result in the modification of products, as in the case of quieter and less polluting motor vehicles.

It is difficult to measure the real dimension of this technological factor; the best approximation can be obtained by means of four indicators;

The environment as a technological factor limited on the whole.

1. The total pollution control effort can be measured by the private sector's investment expenditure, assuming that this investment more or less covers the categories of technical action described above. (As we saw earlier (table 11), this effort varied between 1.6 and 5.4 per cent of total investment in 1978 and has tended to fall over the course of time.

2. The turnover of manufacturers of pollution control equipment would be a useful indicator of the "add-on" part of pollution abatement technologies. Unfortunately, we have no statistics on this point.

3. R and D expenditure on the environment is a valuable indicator of the technological effort made, even though the result obtained is not measured in this way. Here again, we must make do with partial information since we only have statistics on public funding of R and D in this area (Table 4): in 1980, this was still not more than 1 to 3 per cent of total public R and D expenditure. Private financing of R and D, together with the specific part of this financing allotted to the development of clean technologies, is still an unknown. At micro-economic level, the industrial case studies indicate, however, that the industries which have proved most innovative in the environmental field devoted a large share of their R and D budget to this end; but in certain cases this was a short-lived episode (see above and Table 18).

4. Although the three preceding indicators can give an approximate idea of the technological effort

Small penetration
of clean
technologies.

made, they do not in any way measure technological innovation in the environmental field. Such innovation might be approached by a "coefficient of penetration by clean technologies": for example, the percentage of pollution abatement investment spent on developping these clean technologies.

It must be noted however that although the introduction of clean technologies is usually the outcome of an innovation, this "measurement" of innovation is not fully satisfactory: add on technologies may also be innovative and may be necessary when no alternative is available.

In the United States, over the period 1973-1980, industry apparently invested about 20 per cent of its air and water pollution abatement expenditure in changes in production processes (Table 16). Note also that this share has not varied in time. In other words, 80 per cent of all pollution abatement investment consisted of end-of-line treatment, which represents a fairly small penetration by clean technologies.

In France, the penetration of clean technologies has been estimated according to the percentage of industrial plants which have introduced them. With one or two exceptions (57), penetration is small here too (Table 18); thus, in the industries which have made most changes, such as mechanical engineering, only 1.2 per cent of all plants are affected (49). Unfortunately, we do not have comparable statistics for other countries. In Danemark, about one third of firms adopted new production processes for pollution abatement between 1975 and 1980.

A substantial effort
must be made to
broadcast clean
technologies.

In any event, this limited information elicits two obsevations: first, the environment is on the whole a technological factor of limited importance but it can lead to important technical changes in certain industrial sectors, as indicated notably by the industrial case studies. Secondly, judging by the information available on the penetration of clean technologies, technological innovation is still inadequate; on the other hand, the industrial case studies and the clean technology surveys carried out in various countries and at international level (ECE/UN) demonstrate the existence of a large innovation potential and above all a great need for the diffusion of innovation. In many cases, new technologies have already been developed but have not yet spread very far through the industrial fabric. There is thus every advantage in designing and applying environmental policies to

Table 16

Expenditure (US$ million) on new plant and equipment by US industry for air and water pollution abatement by changes in production processes

	1973 Total Air & Water (US$m)	1973 %	1974 Total Air & Water US$m)	1974 %	1975 Total Air & Water (US$m)	1975 %	1976 Total Air & Water (US$m)	1976 %
ALL INDUSTRIES	1,169	100	1,094	100	1,132	100	1,238	100
MANUFACTURING	712	61	540	49	734	65	892	72
DURABLE GOODS	321	27	335	31	272	24	218	18
Primary metals	112	10	137	13	123	11	124	10
Blast furnaces	75	6	36	3	29	3	73	6
Non-ferrous metals	29	2	95	9	85	8	35	3
Electrical machinery,	35	3	83	8	38	3	32	3
Machinery except electrical	36	3	14	1	8	1	6	0
Transport equipment	37	3	17	2	9	1	14	1
Motor vehicles	35	3	10	1	6	1	10	1
Aircraft*	*	*	7	1	3	0	3	0
Stone, clay and glass	50	4	44	4	51	5	14	1
Other durables	52	4	41	4	43	4	28	2
NON-DURABLE GOODS	391	33	205	19	462	41	674	54
Food, including beverages	49	4	18	2	28	2	35	3
Textiles	11	1	3	0	4	0	2	0
Paper	14	1	7	1	26	2	100	8
Chemicals	149	13	67	6	123	11	188	15
Oil	151	13	102	9	276	24	343	28
Rubber	12	1	6	1	5	0	*	*
Other non-durables	5	0	2	0	2	0	6	0
OTHERS INDUSTRIES (NON MANUFACTURING)	457	39	555	51	398	35	346	28
Mining	20	2	11	1	19	2	16	1
Railways	5	0	6	1	5	0	5	0
Air Transport	2	0	2	0	*	*	3	0
Other transport	4	0	8	1	8	1	4	0
Public Utilities	386	33	485	44	334	30	274	22
Electricity	372	32	469	43	314	28	255	21
Gas and other	14	1	16	1	20	2	19	2
Communications, commerce, etc,	41	4	43	4	32	3	45	4

Source: Survey of Current Business, US. Department of Commerce, June, 1980.

Table 16 (condt)

Expenditure (US$ million) on new plant and equipment by US industry
for air and water pollution abatement by changes in production processes

	1977		1978		1979		1980	
	Total Air & Water (US$m)	%	Total Air & Water (US$m)	%	Total Air & Water (US$m)	%	Total Air & Water (US$m)	%
ALL INDUSTRIES	1,330	100	1,376	100	1,317	100	1,324	100
MANUFACTURING	885	67	719	52	687	52	830	63
DURABLES GOODS	259	19	267	19	279	21	367	28
Primary Metals	136	10	130	9	87	7	117	9
Blast furnaces	74	6	77	6	25	2	20	2
Non-ferrous metals	45	3	42	3	48	4	84	6
Electrical machinery	9	1	14	1	20	2	22	2
Machinery except electrical,	12	1	14	1	9	1	14	1
Transport equipment	52	4	73	5	106	8	137	10
Motor vehicles	49	4	67	5	96	7	126	10
Aircraft*	3	0	5	0	7	1	8	1
Stone, clay and glass	13	1	10	1	22	2	31	3
Other durables	37	3	28	2	35	3	43	3
NON-DURABLE GOODS	625	47	453	33	408	31	463	35
Food, including beverages	44	3	53	4	56	4	49	4
Textiles	3	0	10	1	14	1	16	1
Paper	104	8	24	2	37	3	66	5
Chemicals	157	12	88	6	53	4	78	6
Oil	308	23	268	19	235	18	240	18
Rubber	6	0	4	0	3	0	6	0
Other non-durables	4	0	5	0	9	1	7	1
OTHER INDUSTRIES (NON MANUFACTURING)	445	33	655	48	630	48	494	37
Mining	15	1	39	3	34	3	26	2
Railways	1	0	4	0	0	0	0	0
Air Transport	3	0	1	0	2	0	1	0
Other transport	1	0	10	1	7	1	14	1
Public Utilities	378	28	557	40	546	41	408	31
Electricity	364	27	540	39	532	40	394	30
Gas and other	14	1	17	1	14	1	14	1
Communications, commerce, etc,	47	4	45	3	41	3	44	3

Source: Survey of Current Business, US. Department of Commerce, June, 1980.

Table 17

DIFFUSION OF CLEAN TECHNOLOGIES IN THE VARIOUS INDUSTRIES
IN FRANCE

Industry	Research %	Clean processes %	Clean plants %	Clean plants as a percentage of the total number of plants in the industry (1)
Agriculture, animal husbandry	6	3.0	1.5	0.79
Gas, electricity	2	4.0	4.0	72.7
Oil	-	3.0	1.5	5.4
Coal and coke	2	1.0	0.5	1.3
Building materials	6	3.0	5.0	1.9
Metal ore mining, steelmaking, other metals	10	7.0	7.0	2.3
Smelting, metal products	8	11.0	17.0	1.6
Mechanical engineering	6	5.0	19.0	1.2
Glass	-	-	-	-
Chemicals, pharmaceuticals, plastics	20	16.0	14.0	2.6
Agrifood	8	10.5	7.0	0.3
Paper and board	12	4.0	10.5	7.0
Wood	-	3.0	2.0	36.0
Textiles and clothing	6	4.0	6.0	1.7
Leather	4	3.0	7.5	6.1
Other industries	10	13.0	7.0	-
TOTAL.........	100	100	100	100

(1) Calculated according to the number of plants in the industry subject to the pollution charge.

Source : Information collected by the SEDES and quoted by M. Potier and F. Sireyjol, 1981.

facilitate further penetration by technical change (see below).

b)   Nature of this phenomenon

One of the main questions raised during this study concerns the nature of the impact of the environmental regulations on technical change, distinguishing between positive and negative impact. The industrial case studies have helped to identify these two categories of impact, which we sum up below (also see Table 18).

Positive impact on technical change

In the cases studied, the introduction of clean technologies has usually had a positive result for the firm, due mainly to:

The dividends (sometimes unexpected) of clean technologies.

--   improved production processes accompanied by savings in energy and raw materials. In France, a survey of 200 clean technologies (58) shows that in nearly half of the cases examined these technologies have had positive repercussions not initially bargained for: energy savings (51 per cent of all cases), savings in raw materials (47 per cent of all cases) and improved working conditions (40 per cent of all cases). At the same time, certain industrial case studies show that the new production technologies introduced have either considerably reduced the cost of pollution abatement as compared with more traditional technologies or resulted in a net profit in terms of production costs;

-    a saving on pollution control costs, thereby creating good financial conditions for innovation. Thus, in Denmark, it is estimated that in 44 per cent of cases the adoptrion of clean technologies yielded, a financial benefit, which averaged, 12.6 per cent of the investment;

--   the marketing, and therefore the diffusion, of new processes and technologies.

Negative impact on technical change

In the industries studied, far from providing economic or technological benefits, the use of end-of-line treatment processes rather than new production technologies results in higher costs, lower profits and consequently less resources for innovation. At the same time, such processes might

Danger that resources initially intended for "productive" innovation will be diverted.

increase firms' technical rigidity and in the long run reduce their capacity for technical change. Lastly, the adoption of technologies acquired outside puts the firm in a position of technological dependance. Assuming that, as in France and the United States, it is still most common to resort to end-of-line treatment processes, the overall impact of the environment on technical change is rather negative, even though very small on the whole (see above, section 1.2). On the other hand, there may be a significant technical change in the manufacturing of pollution abatement equipment.

When the environmental constraint entails a change in production processes, the technological and economic balance is usually positive. It may happen, however, that when such technical changes are the result of a considerable R and D and investment effort, resources are taken from activities regarded as directly productive or from industrial innovation R and D programmes. It is a fact that in certain cases the large share of the R and D budget allotted to the environment has caused other innovation projects to be cancelled or delayed. However, in most of the cases studied where production processes have been modified, the environment was not the only reason for the technical changes made: the environment modifies or accelerates a programme for improving production processes; pollution abatement often joins the initial objectives of energy and raw material conservation. In France, the above-mentioned survey on clean technologies shows that in 45 per cent of all cases these technologies originally had other objectives than pollution control. Environmental policy should therefore be co-ordinated as far as possible with energy and raw material conservation policy.

The environment is not the only factor giving rise to and orienting innovation.

Much remains to be done for the wider dissemination of technological progress in the environmental field. It must be decided how far environmental policy can contribute to this.

II. CAN ENVIRONMENTAL POLICY FACILITATE TECHNICAL CHANGE ?

2.1. <u>Dialectic between the characteristics of policies and of industries.</u>

Whe have stressed many times that technical change is a complex process involving many variables relating to environmental policies themselves and the firm's own characteristics. These variables, as revealed by the industrial case studies, are summed up in Table 19.

The characteristics of environmental policy can affect technical change during the rule-making process, through the instruments actually used and through enforcement. The case studies enabled us to identify the characteristics which seem most important, and these are summed up below in section 2.2.

The characteristics of the industries concerned must be considered, especially :

An important lesson drawn from this study is the usefulness of adjusting policy to the individual characteristics of the industries concerned. Thus, the industrial cases studies showed that the occurrence, extent and direction of technical change in industry are the result of a rather subtle dialectic between the nature of the policy adopted and the characteristics of the industries concerned. Not only is environmental policy by no means the sole factor, nor the most important one, affecting technical change, but an impact, if there be any, also depends on industries'' own character. These characteristics have been described above (Part Three); they are relatively numerous and one may well question the validity and realism of "made-to-measure" policies tailored to each particular case, especially as technical change is by no means the goal of environmental policy and this adjustment process might come up against contradictory targets and get tied up in inextricable difficulties.

In view of this, the selection of key variables can help the decision-maker to stimulate technical change if necessary. The available information indicates that three characteristics of industries have a decisive impact on technical change.

The firm's innovative capacity...

a) First, there is the firm's innovative capacity and innovation strategy. It is usually when the firm reveals a dynamic innovation strategy or has already launched into a process of technical change that the environmental constraint stimulates an innovatory technological response which in fact becomes part of a technological activity and guides it in a direction compatible with environmental objectives. All things considered, technical change occurs first in firms which are accustomed to controlling it and have the ability and desire to do so; the environment is then only another, albeit important, factor.

Firms with a small innovative capacity are usually ill-equipped to make an effective technological response so that various forms of technological and financial aid and incentives are needed.

...its economic position and investment programmes...

b) The second essential characteristic is the firm's economic position. An abundant cash flow and prospects of growth not only enable it to finance R and D in new technologies but can increase its propensity to take risks. Furthermore, when an investment programme is under way or starting up, experience shows that the effectiveness of pollution control will be all the greater if it is taken into account at an early stage in that programme. Hence the importance of environmental policies which as far as possible enable firms to take appropriate action in advance to comply with pollution abatement constraints (for example, through government-industry consultation and early announcement of the regulations). The industrial case studies have also shown that during a recession even firms with a substantial technological capacity slowed down their innovation policy considerably. The government must therefore take over during a difficult phase and must above all introduce appropriate mechanisms to fund innovation (see below).

...its size and its place in the industry.

c) Lastly, important factors are the size of the firm and the structure of the industry concerned. Although it is not possible to generalise, it must be admitted that, in all the industries studied, the most dynamic firms from the technological viewpoint are large units. The diffusion of technical change is more difficult when an industry consists of small units, but the existence of a few large firms facilitates its penetration.

In these circumstances, since environmental policy must as far as possible take account of firms' internal characteristics, what apportunities are there for action by the government ?

2.2. Government means of action

a) Policy instruments

Emission standards often make more or less specific and constraining references to pollution control technologies which have implicit or explicit government approval. Some form of technological reference in the regulations cannot of course be avoided since, as we have already pointed out, economic realism largely stems fro technological realism: no one is obliged to comply with the impossible. However, in technical matters, the frontiers of the impossible are not always permanent and are in any event constantly receding; nothing could be more prejudicial to technical change than to lay them down beforehand. With no intention of being paradoxical, one could say that an essential teaching of this study is that the less the regulations concern themselves with technology, the more they facilitate technical change. In other words, there is no surer way of inhibiting innovation than to impose ready-made technical solutions on industry. What might be called "technological flexibility" is in our view a fundamental policy rule.

In the examples studied, innovation is always the offspring of innovators' freedom of action. Consequently, whatever the environmental policy instruments may be, if the aim is to encourage technical change (which, once again, is not necessarily the object in view), no technological rule must be dictated. The use of "technological standards" is not always advisable in this connection. The performance standard is usually more effective than the process standard (1). However, this general rule should be qualified in the light of the characteristics of the firms concerned.

A certain guidance may
be necessary for firms
less open to
technical change.

For instance, "technological flexibility" is particularly well-suited to firms which engage in considerable technological activity. In such cases, experience shows that a combination of strict performance standards with freedom of choice of technology and sufficient time gives the best results. On the other hand, a certain technological impetus may be necessary for technologically "rigid" firms disinclined to innovate: the government can suggest more or less forcibly that they use certain technologies and can in any event provide sufficient information on available technologies. This applies particularly to SMEs, which may be in need of real technological assistance.

Finally, there are useful flexible solutions such as the "bubble" concept or the exchange of pollution rights. As a rule, economic incentives, especially pollution charges, have both the advantages of flexibility and of constant stimulus.

There is also the potential role that could be played by government procurement policy geared to new products or equipment.

b)   Enforcement procedures

*Much depends on the
way the regulations
are enforced...*

The analysis of Member countries' environmental policies and the industrial case studies shows that policy enforcement procedures play an essential part in stimulating or inhibiting technological progress. It is at this level that we find an important aspect of the argument between regulation and "deregulation": certain regulations may prove harmful, expensive or inefficient, and it is then the flexibility and efficiency of their enforcement which are most important. A velvet glove is needed between the invisible hand and the iron hand, which is a very good metaphor for the concept of "technological flexibility" mentioned earlier. In this spirit, the government can use four powerful means of action: time, money, information and communication.

Time

*...through flexible
management of time...*

Technical change takes time. Time-limits that are too short and rushed schedules are usually counter-productive. On the other hand, horizons which are too vague are a factor of uncertainty or a bonus for inactivity. The government must aim right and balance its time management at several levels: (i) during the rule-making process, especially so that industry can co-ordinate its investment plans effectively with the pollution controls; (ii) by setting an enforcement schedule, i.e. for the time industry is allowed to comply with the regulations; as already pointed out, this schedule must be adjusted to firms' characteristics: for example, a flexible schedule and a strict standard, or a shorter schedule and a less stringent standard. A distinction should also be made between big firms and SMEs, as well as between industries whose investment time horizons differ, such as heavy industry or the motor vehicle industry, which cover several decades, and other industries whose investment horizon is less than ten years; (iii) through the rapidity and efficiency of administrative procedures (licence applications); and, lastly, (iv) through the period of validity of the licences granted.

Money

A weak financial capacity is a major obstacle to technical change, both for the installation of existing technologies or the funding of R and D. Programmes of financial aid for pollution control can therefore be administered so as to stimulate innovation rather than known but inefficient solutions. Aid for R and D can induce industry to "take the plunge" and shoulder full responsibility for the risks inherent in innovation. In the environmental field, technical change appears to penetrate large production units better than SMEs. Financial aid for innovation in SMEs should be a powerful means of stimulating and diffusing technical change. Collective R and D institutes provide a useful means of promoting technological know-how in SMEs. These bodies are also the ideal intermediary for talking with the regulatory authorities, which can provide them with direct financial aid or sign research contracts with them. Certain forms of financial aid must also be prevented from inhibiting technical change : for instance, aid for the efficient operation of water treatment plant is a counter-incentive to changing production processes ; the various forms of financial aid must therefore be co-ordinated, within the limits set by the application of the Polluter Pays Principle.

...ensuring that sources of finance exist for innovation

Information

The provision of technical information is a decisive factor for technical change. Even though environmental policies have already existed for some ten years, not many people know about treatment methods and "clean technologies". Policy objectives also evolve, just like technologies. In some of the industries studied, lack of technological information has been a definite obstacle to innovation. The State can play a very important role here, especially on behalf of SMEs, by deploying such means as frequent meetings between private and public research bodies, proper training for engineers and technicians, publication of "catalogues" of clean technologies, industry contracts incorporating an R and D clause and the provision of information, exhibition fairs for marketing new technologies and, finally, international co-operation with the exchange of information and common R and D activities. Information also comes from research, and the government has all the more room for action here since public funding of environmental R and D is still small (from 1 to 3 per cent of total public R and D expenditure, according to the country).

...and wide distribution of information.

Consultation

In policy matters there can be no flexibility without dialogue and consultation. The management of time and money and the promotion of technological information are channelled through a continuing dialogue between industry and government, whether during policy-making or during daily policy enforcement in the field. As a rule, industry's reaction is positive when environmental constraints and the technological solutions are discussed in common.

Find a concerted rather than a conflictual approach.

Consultation may be spontaneous when licences are negotiated with industry or it may take place through special mechanisms and institutions. Whatever form it takes, it must prevent or resolve any conflictual relations between the State and industry, which are usually prejudicial to innovation.

These are in our view the main means which the government can use to implement environmental policies in a way which is conducive to technological progress. This does not rule out other means. Above all, it must not relegate the prime objectives of environmental conservation to the background.

2.3. Some facts for the future

It is often asserted that environmental policies are entering a new phase characterised by among other things, a context of slow economic growth accompanied by an increased demand for the "quality of life"; the end of catching-up periods for "first generation pollutants" (in particular sulphur oxides and oxidisable matter); the need to control numerous toxic substances released into the air, soil and water; the challenge and the proliferation of major technological hazards; and finally, the necessity to implement technologies and management practices adapted to the needs of developing countries (60, 61).

This emergence of new issues and aspirations within a difficult economic context makes the development of ever more efficient and adapted solutions all the more necessary.

In particular, this "second generation" of environmental policies coincides with a rapid technological evolution characterised by break through in informatics and the emergence of biotechnologies. These new technologies may constitute a new challenge for environment (in particular biotechnologies); they can also contribute to technical change in the field of environment: non-polluting production processes and new treatment technologies should result from this convergence between on-going technical changes and emerging new environmental policies.

Thus, technical change may turn out to become increasingly an essential part of environmental protection. Public authorities have an important role to play in the management of this evolution for the best environmental protection.

Table 18

SUMMARY OF THE INDUSTRIAL CASE STUDIES

TO = Turnover
CPP = Change of production process
TC = Technical change

CASE	TECHNOLOGICAL RESPONSE	ADVANTAGES	COSTS AND DISADVANTAGES	ENVIRONMENTAL IMPACT ON TC
SUGAR (U.K.)	Small internal changes	–	–	Neutral
(Netherlands)	Sugar recovery and anaerobic waste water treatment	20,000 tonnes/year of sugar recovered (2 per cent of TO), sale of recovered methane gas – saving on pollution charges (14 per cent of TO)	Investments : 7.5 per cent total investment over 11 years, 45 per cent of the R & D budget, no negative impact on TC	Positive – better knowledge and improvement of production processes – environment as accelerator of TC
LEATHER (Netherlands)	Chromium separation (add on) protein separation (add on) chromium recycling (CPP)	Saving on pollution charges and lower treatment costs	Almost made up by savings more than made up in the case of chromium recycling	Positive, but still not widespread ; greater opening to TC
FERTILISERS (Norway)	Waste water recycling	Lower treatment costs	No negative impact on TC	Positive for pollution control, neutral otherwise
ALUMINIUM (Norway)	New dry scrubbing system – recovery of fluoride	Lower energy consumption, improved treatment efficiency	15 per cent of total investment over 5 years No negative impact on TC	Positive for pollution control, neutral otherwise Environment incorporated in already started TC
FERRO-ALLOYS (Norways)	Closed furnace technique ; new air purification methods	Overall reduction in production costs – energy recovery	High but decreasing investment (2.7 per cent of TO in 1976 – 0.75 per cent in 1980) Some investments dropped	Positive – environment as accelerator – improved production process but mechanisation investment stopped.
CEMENT (Norway)	Incineration of hazardous waste	30 per cent energy saving, 6 per cent saving on production costs	No disadvantages	Positive – environment as main cause of CPP
PAPER PULP (France)	In most cases, end-of-line treatment – a few minor changes in production processes	Improved knowledge of production technology – rationalisation	Cost : 3 to 7 per cent of production costs investment: 10 per cent of total investment fewer future investment possibilities for CPP	Rather neutral – positive but limited for certain firms
(United Kingdom)	Fibre recovery – water recycling – end-of-line technologies	Higher profits in the case of fibre recovery	Costs : 0.5 to 5 per cent of TO investment : 10 per cent of total investment, lower profitability and competitiveness	Generally negative – slightly positive in the case of fibre recovery
(Norway and Sweden)	Many TC, e.g. new oxygen bleaching technology and lower emissions of SO_2 – CPP water in closed circuit.Industry reorganised with improved treatment efficiency	Profitability up by 0.2 to 0.7 per cent of TO in the case of oxygen bleaching – recovery of chemicals, energy and fibres	High capital cost of reorganisation. Production overcapacity Sweden : investment (1970–1979) = 13 per cent Cost= 2 to 3 per cent of TO	Positive – leading role of environmental policy

96

Table 18

SUMMARY OF THE INDUSTRIAL CASE STUDIES (condt)

CASE	TECHNOLOGICAL RESPONSE	ADVANTAGES	COSTS AND DISADVANTAGES	ENVIRONMENTAL IMPACT ON TC
(Canada)	Mainly many CPP, closed-circuit production, new pulp production process	Recovery of raw materials, energy and chemicals Improved treatment efficiency Lower pollution control costs	High costs – diversion of R & D resources Firm A : R & D expenditure = 30 per cent of the total, investment = 10 per cent of the total. Firm B : R & D = 20 per cent Investment = 3 per cent (very little diversion of resources)	Positive – environment accelerator of TC.
METAL PLATING (United Kingdom)	Variety of responses – 1970 : CPP and add on 1980 : add on only	Lower production costs in the case of CPP	Certain firms closed down	Small
(Germany)	Mainly add on	Water recycling	No notable negative impact	Small
(France)	As a rule, add-on technologies – a few CPP	Raw material savings – lower production costs – improved working conditions in the case of CPP	No notable negative impact	Small – some diffusion of TC
MOTOR VEHICLES (Europe)	Ready adjustment to pollution and noise standards	Export possibilities	Low costs : R & D : about 10 per cent	Neutral – environment a marginal factor compared with energy savings

Table 19 -   MAIN CHARACTERISTICS OF THE ENVIRONMENTAL   TC= Technical change
              POLICIES AND INDUSTRIES STUDIED   CPP= Change of production process
                                                          TO= Turnover

CASE	INDUSTRY CHARACTERISTICS	POLICY CHARACTERISTICS
SUGAR (United Kingdom)	Old plant	Flexible and pragmatic enforcement
(Netherlands)	Positive attitude - economic and technological dynamism - modernisation programme - CPP - large firm	High and increasing pollution charges - technological flexibility - consultation - aid for R & D.
LEATHER	Low receptiveness to the environment and TC - resistance to change - poor economic position - small firms	High pollution charges - uncertainty - unco-ordinated regulations - economic aid tied to compliance with the environmental regulations
FERRO-ALLOYS (Norway)	Dynamic innovation strategy - high receptiveness to the environment - initially favourable economic position	Technological flexibility - time allowed for innovation - consultation
FERTILISERS (Norway)	Large firm - substantial R & D activity (0.14 per cent of TO) - environment incorporated in an overall CPP programme - positive attitude	Technological flexibility - consultation - pragmatic enforcement
ALUMINIUM (Norway)	Large firm - substantial R & D activity (0.6 per cent of TO) - environment incorporated in an overall CPP programme - positive attitude	Technological flexibility - severe standards
CEMENT (Norway)	Large firm - substantial investment	Technological flexibility - consultation and common R & D - financial aid
PAPER PULP (France)	Two types of firm : (1) poor economic position, resistance to TC, negative attitude - add-on technologies ; (2) better economic position, integration in a group, technological dynamism, CPP	Technological flexibility but time-limits too strict - financial aid for investment (51 per cent) - no provision of technical information
(United Kingdom)	Bad economic position - cautious technological activity	Technological flexibility - pragmatism - consultation - provision of information
(Norway and Sweden)	Substantial R & D activity - open attitude to TC - concentrated industry	Technological flexibility - strict standards - substantial financial aid. In Sweden, the much too brief compliance period and a short-term programme of financial aid have fostered add-on technologies rather than CPP.
(Canada)	Old industry - substantial R & D activity - environment incorporated in a CPP programme - positive attitude - large firms.	Technological flexibility - strict standards - strict time-limits.
METAL-PLATING (United Kingdom)	Very disparate industry - deterioration of the economic position in 1980 - two types of firm : (1) large firms, positive attitude, good technical information, CPP ; (2) small firms, resistance to TC, no technical information, add-on technology.	Flexibility - adjustment according to firms' individual position - need for the provision of technical information and incentives for TC.
(France)	Small firms : technological rigidity - little opening to CPP Big firms : open to TC and CPP - positive attitude to the environment - better financial position.	Flexibility - consultation - provision of technical information - pollution charges - financial aid.
(Germany)	Technological rigidity - no technical information - uncompetitive market - no CPP	Consultation - financial aid for end-of-line treatment
MOTOR VEHICLES (Europe)	Key sector of the economy - large firms - heavy exporters - substantial technological activity - heavy competition.	Caution and flexibility in manufacturing countries - negotiations with industry - standards negotiated at international level - State aid for for R & D.

FOOTNOTES AND REFERENCES

1. OECD, Science and Technology Policy for the 1980s. Paris, 1981.

2. Denison E.F. (1979) Accounting for Slower Economic Growth. The Brookings Institution. Washington D.C.

3. The fact that this -0.7 per cent is greater than the -0.6 per cent annual average is explained by the fact that other factors had a positive effect.

4. OECD, Macro Economic Impact of Environmental Policies. Paris 1985.

5. OECD, Technical Change and Economic Policy. Paris 1980.
   See also OECD: OECD Science and Technology Indicators. Paris 1984.

6. Christainsen G. and Haveman R., "Public Regulation and the Slowdown in Productivity Growth" American Economic Review - N° 320 May 1981.

7. Over this period the productivity growth rate fell 1.3 percentage points. Christainsen and Haveman made their calculations on the basis of "regulatory intensity" indices.

8. Christainsen G. and Haveman R. "Environmental Regulation and Productivity Growth" in Environmental Regulation and the U.S. Economy" - Edited by H.M. Peskin, P.R. Portney, A.V.Kneese - Resources for the Future - Washington - 1981.

9. Christainsen and Haveman nevertheless stress the very approximate nature of these figures. A comparitive assessment of the studies on environment and productivity can be found in Christainsen and Haveman (8) and OECD (4).

10. Gaudin T. et Aubert J.E., "Le sens de l'innovation". Le Progrès Technique n°19 - Paris, 1980.

11. The complexity of the phenomena involved rules out any exhaustive discussion here. For an in-depth analysis see inter alia: OECD (1, 5, 12) and Rothwell and Zegveld (13).

12. Cf. OECD : The Welfare State in Crisis - Paris 1981.

13. Rothwell R. and Zegveld W. Industrial Innovation and Public Policy - Frances Printers - London 1981.

14. Freeman C., Industrial Innovation - Penguin Books 1974.

15.   For a study of the causes of this decline see OECD (1).

16.   OECD, Innovation in small and medium firms. Paris, 1982.

17.   Gaudin T. "Les obstacles à l'innovation", Le Progrès Technique n°18, 1980.

18.   OECD, Public expenditures Trends, Paris 1978.

19.   For example, the "Federal Register" of the United States where all federal regulations are published, from a size of 3,500 pages in the year 1937, increased to 35 000 pages in 1973, 60 000 in 1975 and 85 000 in 1980, i.e. an annual growth rate of 7.6 per cent between 1960 and 1965 and of 14 per cent between 1974 and 1979 (Economic Report of the President - 1982).

20.   Chamber of Commerce of the United States Government Regulation of Business: its Growth, Impact and Future, 1979.

21.   Economic Council of Canada. Reforming Regulation. Ottawa 1981.

22.   Hill C.T. et Utterback J.M., Technological Innovation for a Dynamic Economy - Pergamon Press 1979.

23.   Chamber of Commerce of the United States (20) and Weidenbaum, MC. Cost of Regulations and the Benefit of Reform. Center for the Study of American Business, Washington UIniversity, St-Louis, 1979.

24.   Du Pont, for example, the american firm with the biggest R and D programme, has estimated that its R and D expenditure devoted to marketed products (reformulation and modification of processes) has increased from about two thirds to almost three quarters over the past ten years, this developent being attributed to such factors as the costs of energy and raw material and competition. (Chemical and Engineering News, 3rd October, 1977). See also OECD: Regulation and Innovation in the Chemical Industry: A preliminary Assessment of the Impact of Recent Chemicals Legislation, Paris 1982.

25.   OECD, The Impact of Chemicals Control upon Trade, Innovation and the Small Firm. Paris 1982.

26.   Firms ranking lower than the 20 biggest accounted for 2.2 per cent of the manufacture of new products during the period 1967-71 as against 6.9 per cent in 1957-61.

27.   In the United States, the practice of marketable pollution rights is developping in the frame of EPA's "Emission Trading Program".

28.   On this subject, see among others the survey of clean technologies carried out by the ECE, Geneva and "Les Techniques Propres dans l'Industrie Française", Ministère de l'Environnement - Paris 1981.

29.   Ministry of the Environnement (France). Données économiques de l'environnement, Paris 1980.

30. Pulp and paper, sugar, metal plating, leather tanning, potato starch, ferro aloys, aluminium, fertilizers, cement and the motor vehicle industry.

31. OECD, Environmental Policy in Sweden Paris 1977.

32. Harvard Law Review "Rethinking Regulation: Negociation as an Alternative to Traditional Rulemaking", Vol. 94, June 1981.

33. Safety in a collision.

34. Financial aid could only be obtained in exchange for pollution abatement measures.

35. In fact, the polluter endeavours to reduce the total cost made up of the cost of treatment and the charge paid (see OECD). Pollution Charges in Practice, Paris 1980.

36. A detailed study will be found in OECD, Pollution Charges in Practice and Brashares E.N., Harrington CN, Magat W.A., Peskin A.M. Industrial Air and Water Pollution Regulations and Innovation - Ressources for the future - Washington D.C. 1979.

37. See OECD, The Influence of Technology in Determining Emission and Effluent Standards, Paris 1979.

38. Witness the results of the notification procedure for the financial aid systems for pollution prevention and control.

39. It was estimated in 1975 that 80 per cent of total government aid for R and D went to big firms (over 25 000 employees) in the United States; in France, the 20 largest firms received 90 per cent of these funds (OECD, - 16 -)

40. An analysis of these policies will be found in Rothwell and Zegveld, (13).

41. In the United States, the ETIP study mentioned above, recommends for example, a "value incentive clause" whereby the manufacturer shares with the government the benefits of an innovation benefiting to the public sector; See Experimental Technology Incentives Program (ETIP) Taxonomy of Incentives Approaches for Stimulating Innovation, National Bureau of Standards - Washington DC. 1979.

42. According to Rothwell and Zegveld (op. cit. 1981), Government procurement policies have the following general aims :

    1. to improve the quality of the products uses by the public sector ;

    2. to improve the quality of the products uses by the private sector in the light of certain objectives ;

    3. to improve the international competitiveness of domestic enterprises.

43. European Communities: "Le Poids du Secteur Public" 30 jours d'Europe OECD - 1981.

44. Bizaguet, A. "Les Nationalisations" - Revue Economique n°3, Paris Mai 1983.

45. This part of the analysis is based essentially on the investigations into a number of specific industries.

46. Abernathy W.J. The Productivity Dilemma. John Hopkins-University Press, Baltimore, 1979.

47. J.M. Utterback (1979) "The Dynamics of Product and Process Innovation". In C.T. Hill, J.M. Utterback (1979) (Eds.), Technological Innovation for a Dynamic Economy. Pergammon Press. New-York

    Weidenbaum M.L., Costs of regulation and the benefits of reform - Center for the Study of American Business, Washington University, St-Louis, 1979.

48. Thus, no firm has adopted the new chromium recycling process (developed by the TNO Research Institute) which would be potentially the most efficient and most economically profitable.

49. Potier M. and Sireyjol, F., "Coûts et avantages des techniques propres" Futuribles n°44 - Paris 1981.

50. Ashford N.A., Heaton G.R., "The Impact of Environmental Protection Regulations on Research and Development in the Industrial Chemical Industry", in C.T. HILL (ed) Federal Regulation and Chemical Innovation. American Chemical Society Symposium Series. Washington D.C. 1979.

51. For example, paper pulp in Canada, Norway and Sweden, sugar in the Netherlands, and cement, aluminium and fertilisers in Norway.

52. The criteria adopted by an American chemicals firm for proving the profitability of prospective pollution abatement schemes fall into this category:

    1. the scheme must reduce or eliminate pollution ;
    2. it must account for savings in energy, raw materials and other resources ;
    3. it must lead to a technological innovation
    4. It mut be financially profitable.

    In terms of industrial logic, the order of these criteria could very well be reversed.

53. For example, the profit from marketing pollution abatement technologies.

54. Krupnick A.J., Yardas D.R., Innovative technology compliance extensions : A qualitative economic analysis of section 301(K) of the 1971 Clean Water Act Amendments, Environmental Policy Evaluation Program, Resources for the Future, Washington D.C., 1981.

55. "Ministerial Declaration on Future Policies for Science and Technology" (OECD, - 1 -).

56. For example, France has set itself the target of raising GERD from 1.8 per cent of GDP in 1980 to 2.5 per cent in 1985.

57. Wood industry and gas and electricity (State monopoly).

58. Ministry of the Environment (France), Environnement et productivité (Miméo) Paris 1982.

59. Which does not invalidate a policy to provide information on existing technologies.

60. Barde J.Ph. and Potier, M. ; "Dix ans de politique de l'environnement" - Futuribles n°26 Paris Sept. 1979.

61. Barré, R. and Godet, O.: Les nouvelles frontières de l'environnement. Economica - Paris 1982.

OECD SALES AGENTS
DÉPOSITAIRES DES PUBLICATIONS DE L'OCDE

ARGENTINA – ARGENTINE
Carlos Hirsch S.R.L., Florida 165, 4° Piso (Galería Guemes)
1333 BUENOS AIRES, Tel. 33.1787.2391 y 30.7122

AUSTRALIA – AUSTRALIE
Australia and New Zealand Book Company Pty, Ltd.,
10 Aquatic Drive, Frenchs Forest, N.S.W. 2086
P.O. Box 459, BROOKVALE, N.S.W. 2100. Tel. (02) 452.44.11

AUSTRIA – AUTRICHE
OECD Publications and Information Center
4 Simrockstrasse 5300 Bonn (Germany). Tel. (0228) 21.60.45
Local Agent/Agent local :
Gerold and Co., Graben 31, WIEN 1. Tel. 52.22.35

BELGIUM – BELGIQUE
Jean De Lannoy, Service Publications OCDE
avenue du Roi 202, B-1060 BRUXELLES. Tel. 02/538.51.69

CANADA
Renouf Publishing Company Limited,
Central Distribution Centre,
61 Sparks Street (Mall),
P.O.B. 1008 - Station B,
OTTAWA, Ont. KIP 5R1.
Tel. (613)238.8985-6
Toll Free: 1-800.267.4164
Librairie Renouf Limitée
980 rue Notre-Dame,
Lachine, P.Q. H8S 2B9,
Tel. (514) 634-7088.

DENMARK – DANEMARK
Munksgaard Export and Subscription Service
35, Nørre Søgade
DK 1370 KØBENHAVN K. Tel. +45.1.12.85.70

FINLAND – FINLANDE
Akateeminen Kirjakauppa
Keskuskatu 1, 00100 HELSINKI 10. Tel. 65.11.22

FRANCE
Bureau des Publications de l'OCDE,
2 rue André-Pascal, 75775 PARIS CEDEX 16. Tel. (1) 524.81.67
Principal correspondant :
13602 AIX-EN-PROVENCE : Librairie de l'Université.
Tel. 26.18.08

GERMANY – ALLEMAGNE
OECD Publications and Information Center
4 Simrockstrasse 5300 BONN (0228) 21.60.45

GREECE – GRÈCE
Librairie Kauffmann, 28 rue du Stade,
ATHÈNES 132. Tel. 322.21.60

HONG-KONG
Government Information Services,
Publications (Sales) Office,
Beaconsfield House, 4/F.,
Queen's Road Central

ICELAND – ISLANDE
Snaebjörn Jönsson and Co., h.f.,
Hafnarstraeti 4 and 9, P.O.B. 1131, REYKJAVIK.
Tel. 13133/14281/11936

INDIA – INDE
Oxford Book and Stationery Co. :
NEW DELHI-1, Scindia House. Tel. 45896
CALCUTTA 700016, 17 Park Street. Tel. 240832

INDONESIA – INDONÉSIE
PDIN-LIPI, P.O. Box 3065/JKT., JAKARTA, Tel. 583467

IRELAND – IRLANDE
TDC Publishers – Library Suppliers
12 North Frederick Street, DUBLIN 1 Tel. 744835-749677

ITALY – ITALIE
Libreria Commissionaria Sansoni :
Via Lamarmora 45, 50121 FIRENZE. Tel. 579751/584468
Via Bartolini 29, 20155 MILANO. Tel. 365083
Sub-depositari :
Ugo Tassi
Via A. Farnese 28, 00192 ROMA. Tel. 310590
Editrice e Libreria Herder,
Piazza Montecitorio 120, 00186 ROMA. Tel. 6794628
Costantino Ercolano, Via Generale Orsini 46, 80132 NAPOLI. Tel. 405210
Libreria Hoepli, Via Hoepli 5, 20121 MILANO. Tel. 865446
Libreria Scientifica, Dott. Lucio de Biasio "Aeiou"
Via Meravigli 16, 20123 MILANO Tel. 807679
Libreria Zanichelli
Piazza Galvani 1/A, 40124 Bologna Tel. 237389
Libreria Lattes, Via Garibaldi 3, 10122 TORINO. Tel. 519274
La diffusione delle edizioni OCSE è inoltre assicurata dalle migliori librerie nelle
città più importanti.

JAPAN – JAPON
OECD Publications and Information Center,
Landic Akasaka Bldg., 2-3-4 Akasaka,
Minato-ku, TOKYO 107 Tel. 586.2016

KOREA – CORÉE
Pan Korea Book Corporation,
P.O. Box n° 101 Kwangwhamun, SÉOUL. Tel. 72.7369

LEBANON – LIBAN
Documenta Scientifica/Redico,
Edison Building, Bliss Street, P.O. Box 5641, BEIRUT.
Tel. 354429 – 344425

MALAYSIA – MALAISIE
University of Malaya Co-operative Bookshop Ltd.
P.O. Box 1127, Jalan Pantai Baru
KUALA LUMPUR. Tel. 577701/577072

THE NETHERLANDS – PAYS-BAS
Staatsuitgeverij, Verzendboekhandel,
Chr. Plantijnstraat 1 Postbus 20014
2500 EA S-GRAVENHAGE. Tel. nr. 070.789911
Voor bestellingen: Tel. 070.789208

NEW ZEALAND – NOUVELLE-ZÉLANDE
Publications Section,
Government Printing Office Bookshops:
AUCKLAND: Retail Bookshop: 25 Rutland Street,
Mail Orders: 85 Beach Road, Private Bag C.P.O.
HAMILTON: Retail: Ward Street,
Mail Orders, P.O. Box 857
WELLINGTON: Retail: Mulgrave Street (Head Office),
Cubacade World Trade Centre
Mail Orders: Private Bag
CHRISTCHURCH: Retail: 159 Hereford Street,
Mail Orders: Private Bag
DUNEDIN: Retail: Princes Street
Mail Order: P.O. Box 1104

NORWAY – NORVÈGE
J.G. TANUM A/S
P.O. Box 1177 Sentrum OSLO 1. Tel. (02) 80.12.60

PAKISTAN
Mirza Book Agency, 65 Shahrah Quaid-E-Azam, LAHORE 3.
Tel. 66839

PORTUGAL
Livraria Portugal, Rua do Carmo 70-74,
1117 LISBOA CODEX. Tel. 360582/3

SINGAPORE – SINGAPOUR
Information Publications Pte Ltd,
Pei-Fu Industrial Building,
24 New Industrial Road N° 02-06
SINGAPORE 1953, Tel. 2831786, 2831798

SPAIN – ESPAGNE
Mundi-Prensa Libros, S.A.
Castelló 37, Apartado 1223, MADRID-28001, Tel. 275.46.55
Libreria Bosch, Ronda Universidad 11, BARCELONA 7.
Tel. 317.53.08, 317.53.58

SWEDEN – SUÈDE
AB CE Fritzes Kungl Hovbokhandel,
Box 16 356, S 103 27 STH, Regeringsgatan 12,
DS STOCKHOLM. Tel. 08/23.89.00
Subscription Agency/Abonnements:
Wennergren-Williams AB,
Box 30004, S104 25 STOCKHOLM.
Tel. 08/54.12.00

SWITZERLAND – SUISSE
OECD Publications and Information Center
4 Simrockstrasse 5300 BONN (Germany). Tel. (0228) 21.60.45
Local Agents/Agents locaux
Librairie Payot, 6 rue Grenus, 1211 GENÈVE 11. Tel. 022.31.89.50

TAIWAN – FORMOSE
Good Faith Worldwide Int'l Co., Ltd.
9th floor, No. 118, Sec. 2,
Chung Hsiao E. Road
TAIPEI. Tel. 391.7396/391.7397

THAILAND – THAILANDE
Suksit Siam Co., Ltd., 1715 Rama IV Rd,
Samyan, BANGKOK 5. Tel. 2511630

TURKEY – TURQUIE
Kültur Yayinlari Is-Türk Ltd. Sti.
Atatürk Bulvari No : 191/Kat. 21
Kavaklidere/ANKARA. Tel. 17 02 66
Dolmabahce Cad. No : 29
BESIKTAS/ISTANBUL. Tel. 60 71 88

UNITED KINGDOM – ROYAUME-UNI
H.M. Stationery Office,
P.O.B. 276, LONDON SW8 5DT.
(postal orders only)
Telephone orders: (01) 622.3316, or
49 High Holborn, LONDON WC1V 6 HB (personal callers)
Branches at: EDINBURGH, BIRMINGHAM, BRISTOL,
MANCHESTER, BELFAST.

UNITED STATES OF AMERICA – ÉTATS-UNIS
OECD Publications and Information Center, Suite 1207,
1750 Pennsylvania Ave., N.W. WASHINGTON, D.C.20006 – 4582
Tel. (202) 724.1857

VENEZUELA
Libreria del Este, Avda. F. Miranda 52, Edificio Galipan,
CARACAS 106. Tel. 32.23.01/33.26.04/31.58.38

YUGOSLAVIA – YOUGOSLAVIE
Jugoslovenska Knjiga, Knez Mihajlova 2, P.O.B. 36, BEOGRAD.
Tel. 621.992

Les commandes provenant de pays où l'OCDE n'a pas encore désigné de dépositaire peuvent être adressées à :
OCDE, Bureau des Publications, 2, rue André-Pascal, 75775 PARIS CEDEX 16.
Orders and inquiries from countries where sales agents have not yet been appointed may be sent to:
OECD, Publications Office, 2, rue André-Pascal, 75775 PARIS CEDEX 16.

68656-05-1985

OECD PUBLICATIONS, 2, rue André-Pascal, 75775 PARIS CEDEX 16 - No. 43313 1985
PRINTED IN FRANCE
(97 85 07 1) ISBN 92-64-12731-3

302534569.